Drupal 7 Themes

Create new themes for your Drupal 7 site with a clean
layout and powerful CSS styling

Ric Shreves

open source
community experience distilled

PACKT
PUBLISHING

BIRMINGHAM - MUMBAI

Drupal 7 Themes

First published: May 2011

Production Reference: 1190511

Published by Packt Publishing Ltd.
32 Lincoln Road
Olton
Birmingham, B27 6PA, UK.

ISBN 978-1-849512-76-3

www.packtpub.com

Cover Image by Faustino Perez (faustperez@yahoo.es)

Credits

Author

Ric Shreves

Reviewer

Sivaji Ganesh

Acquisition Editor

Sarah Cullington

Development Editor

Maitreya Bhakal

Technical Editors

Sakina Kaydawala

Prashant Macha

Manasi Poonthottam

Project Coordinator

Joel Goveya

Proofreader

Lynda Sliwoski

Indexer

Hemangini Bari

Production Coordinator

Adline Swetha Jesuthas

Cover Work

Adline Swetha Jesuthas

About the Author

Ric Shreves is one of the founding partners of water&stone, an interactive agency that specializes in open source web content management systems. Ric has been building CMS websites for over 10 years and during that time he has been involved in projects for a number of global brands, including BASF, BearingPoint, Colgate-Palmolive, Tesco Lotus, FPDSavills CBRichard Ellis, Mercy Corps, and many others. Ric has published a number of books on open source in general and on open source content management systems in particular. Past work includes books on Mambo, Drupal, Joomla!, and Ubuntu. This is his third installment in the *Drupal Themes* series for *Packt Publishing*.

Ric lives in Bali with his wife and business partner, Nalisa.

I would like to thank Packt for giving me the opportunity to be a part of the Drupal Themes series; it's been a great experience for me and has taught me a tremendous amount about Drupal—a system for which I have ever-increasing admiration. Writing these books takes a tremendous amount of time; it would not be possible without the continuing support of my wife Nalisa, who keeps things running smoothly at water&stone while I bang away on the keyboard, so I dedicate this book to her and the entire water&stone team.

About the Reviewer

Sivaji Ganesh is one of the lead web developers at E-ndicus InfoTech Pvt Ltd, a leading Drupal and OpenERP services providing organization based in Chennai. At E-ndicus, he is responsible for requirements analysis, arriving at and providing solutions, and building and maintaining websites primarily on Drupal.

In 2009, Sivaji started his Drupal evangelism as Google Summer of Code student. There he worked on quiz module to improve its features and fix several bugs along with other Drupal developers Matt Butcher, Falcon, Vegardjo, and Turadg. He is an active member, who contributed to the community in terms of writing patches to core and contributed modules. He has developed and maintains a few contributed modules and themes on the Drupal official website `http://drupal.org/`. He has reviewed a few other Drupal books for *Packt Publishing*, including *Drupal 7 Module Development*. Sivaji's Drupal user account page can be found at `http://drupal.org/user/328724`.

He holds a Bachelors Degree in Computer Science from Jaya Engineering College, affiliated to Anna University, Chennai.

I would like to extend my sincere thanks to my family and colleagues. Of course to everyone in the Drupal community, who instilled a Drupal-inquisitive mind in me.

www.PacktPub.com

Support files, eBooks, discount offers and more

You might want to visit www.PacktPub.com for support files and downloads related to your book.

Did you know that Packt offers eBook versions of every book published, with PDF and ePub files available? You can upgrade to the eBook version at www.PacktPub.com and as a print book customer, you are entitled to a discount on the eBook copy. Get in touch with us at service@packtpub.com for more details.

At www.PacktPub.com, you can also read a collection of free technical articles, sign up for a range of free newsletters and receive exclusive discounts and offers on Packt books and eBooks.

http://PacktLib.PacktPub.com

Do you need instant solutions to your IT questions? PacktLib is Packt's online digital book library. Here, you can access, read and search across Packt's entire library of books.

Why Subscribe?

- Fully searchable across every book published by Packt
- Copy and paste, print and bookmark content
- On demand and accessible via web browser

Free Access for Packt account holders

If you have an account with Packt at www.PacktPub.com, you can use this to access PacktLib today and view nine entirely free books. Simply use your login credentials for immediate access.

Table of Contents

Preface

Drupal is an award winning open source Content Management System (CMS). Based on PHP and MySQL, its power and flexibility combined with its exceptional design mean it is one of the most popular choices for creating a CMS website.

Drupal employs a specialized templating system and supports themes, which allow you to change the look and feel of your system's front and backend interfaces.

Drupal 7 Themes is an ideal introduction to theming with Drupal 7. If you want to create a striking new look for your Drupal 7 website, this book is for you. This book is a revised, updated, and expanded edition of Drupal 6 Themes, rewritten specifically for Drupal 7.

This book will show you techniques and tools to help you improve the look and feel of any Drupal 7-powered website. Starting from the basics of theme setup and configuration, you will learn about the Drupal theming architecture and the PHPTemplate engine, and then move on to modifying existing themes and building new themes from scratch. You will find out about tools to make your theme development easier.

What this book covers

Chapter 1, The Elements of a Drupal Theme: We begin by introducing how Drupal themes work and by looking at the constituent parts of a typical theme. This chapter builds familiarity with key Drupal theming concepts and lays the groundwork for the chapters that follow.

Chapter 2, Working with the Default Configuration and Display Options: In this chapter, we dig into the opportunities presented by the default theme and display configuration settings included in the Drupal core. The focus is on getting the most out of the default system without having to do any additional customization. This chapter builds fluency with basic concepts by showing the system in action.

Chapter 3, Understanding PHPTemplate Themes: The PHPTemplate theme engine lies at the core of Drupal themes. This chapter explains how it works and looks at how themers can leverage the features of the theme engine to create compliant themes and customize them effectively.

Chapter 4, Using Intercepts and Overrides: Intercepting and overriding theme output is a key concept and one of the most important techniques in Drupal theming. This chapter introduces the concept then teaches you how to apply it. The chapter covers how to apply the technique to templates, functions, styles, and preprocessors.

Chapter 5, Customizing an Existing Theme: This chapter focuses is on sub-theming. The chapter covers how to quickly and easily build a proper sub-theme and then how to use that sub-theme to create a customized look and feel for a Drupal site.

Chapter 6, Creating a New Theme: This chapter shows how to create a new theme for you Drupal 7 site. The contents cover both creation of a new theme through the sub-theming technique and creating a new theme without the benefit of a sub-theme.

Chapter 7, Dynamic Theming: A review of the different techniques available for creating templates and styles that are responsive to the conditions on the screen. The chapter covers how to display templates and styles in response to the content being displayed, or the user viewing the content.

Chapter 8, Theming Drupal Forms: This chapter reviews all of the forms included in the Drupal core, then discusses the range of options available for modifying the output of those forms. The techniques range from basic concepts like modifying styling all the way through the use of custom modules to modify themes.

Chapter 9, Common Challenges in Drupal Theming: This chapter provides a discussion on how to deal with common issues that arise during Drupal theming. Topics range from theming specific types of output to managing accessibility to coping with the small problems that tend to crop up during theme development.

Chapter 10, Useful Extensions for Themers: The final chapter looks at software tools that can aid theme development. The chapter includes a list of Drupal modules that are useful to themers as well as third-party tools that can make the job faster and easier.

Appendix, Indentifying Templates, Stylesheets, and Themable Functions: The book's appendix provides a handy one-stop reference to themable elements of Drupal 7. We list in one place, all the system's stylesheets, templates, and themable functions. The appendix is organized topically and designed to make it easier for you to find the style elements you need without having to dig through the online reference materials to find all the relevant information.

What you need for this book

The most important requirement for getting the most out of this book is access to Drupal 7 installation. It does not matter whether the Drupal site is hosted on an external web host or on a local server. The important point is that you can get access to not only the front and back end, but also to the database and the files.

Addition tools that will allow you to get the most out of this text:

- An FTP program for moving files to and from your Drupal 7 installation
- A code editing program

Who this book is for

The main requirements to make use of this book are knowledge of HTML, CSS, and a touch of creativity. You don't need to know anything about theming in Drupal; all you need is basic experience of working with Drupal.

Although this book aims to make Drupal theming accessible to designers, theming in Drupal 7 involves writing some PHP code, and a basic knowledge of PHP will be helpful.

Regardless of your technical skills, this book will teach you to design themes for your Drupal websites quickly and easily.

Conventions

In this book, you will find a number of styles of text that distinguish between different kinds of information. Here are some examples of these styles, and an explanation of their meaning.

Code words in text are shown as follows: "The next step, therefore, is to open up our new directory and delete everything except `.info`, `/templates/page.tpl.php`, and `template.php`."

A block of code is set as follows:

```
functionjeanb_menu_tree($variables) {
return '<ul class="menu clearfix">' . $variables['tree'] . '</
ul>';
}
```

When we wish to draw your attention to a particular part of a code block, the relevant lines or items are set in bold:

```php
<?php if ($site_slogan);?>
    <div id="site-slogan">
      <?php print $site_slogan; ?>
    </div>
<?php endif; ?>
```

New terms and **important words** are shown in bold. Words that you see on the screen, in menus or dialog boxes for example, appear in the text like this: "Either click the **SETTINGS** tab on the top-right of Theme Manager, or click the **Settings** link below the theme's description."

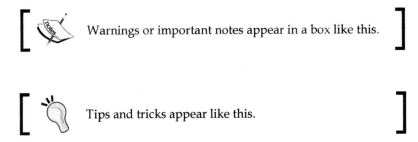

> Warnings or important notes appear in a box like this.

> Tips and tricks appear like this.

Reader feedback

Feedback from our readers is always welcome. Let us know what you think about this book—what you liked or may have disliked. Reader feedback is important for us to develop titles that you really get the most out of.

To send us general feedback, simply send an e-mail to feedback@packtpub.com, and mention the book title via the subject of your message.

If there is a book that you need and would like to see us publish, please send us a note in the **SUGGEST A TITLE** form on www.packtpub.com or e-mail suggest@packtpub.com.

If there is a topic that you have expertise in and you are interested in either writing or contributing to a book, see our author guide on www.packtpub.com/authors.

Customer support

Now that you are the proud owner of a Packt book, we have a number of things to help you to get the most from your purchase.

Errata

Although we have taken every care to ensure the accuracy of our content, mistakes do happen. If you find a mistake in one of our books — maybe a mistake in the text or the code — we would be grateful if you would report this to us. By doing so, you can save other readers from frustration and help us improve subsequent versions of this book. If you find any errata, please report them by visiting http://www.packtpub.com/support, selecting your book, clicking on the **errata submission form** link, and entering the details of your errata. Once your errata are verified, your submission will be accepted and the errata will be uploaded on our website, or added to any list of existing errata, under the Errata section of that title. Any existing errata can be viewed by selecting your title from http://www.packtpub.com/support.

Piracy

Piracy of copyright material on the Internet is an ongoing problem across all media. At Packt, we take the protection of our copyright and licenses very seriously. If you come across any illegal copies of our works, in any form, on the Internet, please provide us with the location address or website name immediately so that we can pursue a remedy.

Please contact us at copyright@packtpub.com with a link to the suspected pirated material.

We appreciate your help in protecting our authors, and our ability to bring you valuable content.

Questions

You can contact us at questions@packtpub.com if you are having a problem with any aspect of the book, and we will do our best to address it.

1
Learning the Basics of Drupal Theming

This chapter introduces the key concepts that underpin the Drupal theming system and explains the role that themes play in the presentation of a site's output.

The chapter covers the various types of themes, the elements of a theme, and the functions those elements fulfill. At the end of the chapter, we will also look at the themes contained in the Drupal distribution and examine exactly what it is that makes each theme distinct.

The contents of this preliminary chapter provide the general comprehension necessary to grasp the big picture of the role of themes in Drupal. Think of the knowledge communicated in this chapter as a foundation upon which to build the skills that follow in the subsequent chapters.

The topics covered in this chapter include:

- The role of themes in the Drupal system
- Basic principles to guide your work
- The relationship between theme files and the theme engine
- The output of the themes for both site visitors and site administrators
- An overview of the default themes

Let's start by looking at the key role themes play in the Drupal system.

The importance of themes in Drupal

The theme employed on your Drupal site defines the visual appearance of the site. The theme files control the placement of the elements on the screen and impact both the presentation of the contents and the usability of the functionality. How well a theme is designed and implemented is, therefore, largely responsible for the first impression made by your site. Themes are the most visible, and arguably the most influential, element of your Drupal site.

While the default Drupal distribution includes a set of themes that will prove sufficient for some users, it is assumed that you are reading this book out of a desire to do more, whether it be only to install additional themes and customize them or to build your own themes.

In order to grasp better some of the challenges (and opportunities) associated with Drupal themes, it is useful to look at four concepts that run throughout this book. These concepts impact the way you will use the system and the way in which you will plan your theme deployment.

The four concepts are:

- One template or many? It's up to you
- Get creative with configuration
- Intercept and override
- Sub-themes are your friends

One template or many? It's up to you

Drupal allows you to implement customizations to your theme at a variety of levels, and thereby provides you with extremely granular control over the appearance of your site. While you do have the option to set a single unified look for the entire site, you also have the option to create visually distinct pages or groups of pages. You can even control the appearance of the individual elements on specific pages, if you so desire.

The Drupal theme system permits you to assign different templates to different purposes on your site. You can, for example, create a nice visual template for use on your home page, then build another suitable for the display of text on your content pages, and yet another for use on your forms pages. Indeed, not only can you specify different templates for different pages, but you also have the ability to provide styling for specific types of content or even for the output of a particular functionality. As you will see later in this chapter, templates can be nested inside each other, giving you the ability to affect the site's look and feel at multiple levels.

The Drupal system is sometimes the subject of criticism due to its perceived complexity. While the system does exhibit a certain degree of complexity, with it comes a great deal of power. Once you develop familiarity with the system and attain a bit of practice, you will discover that the system is very flexible and rewarding. In the following chapters, we will look at how to implement multiple templates and how to theme and configure all the various constituent parts of the Drupal system.

Get creative with configuration

Use Drupal's blocks functionality to impact the presentation layer via thoughtful use of the configuration and placement options.

A great deal of the output you see on the screen of a Drupal site is provided by the system's blocks and modules. The process of activating modules and assigning blocks to the pages is one of the most basic and important skills in Drupal site building. A great deal of flexibility can be squeezed out of the system in this area alone. Understanding the configuration options available for the blocks and modules is one of the keys to building interesting and usable sites.

Modules are standalone bits of code—mini applications in some cases—that extend the functionality of your site. It is through modules that Drupal provides functions like the Forum, the Aggregator, and even additional administration functionality, like the Overlay module.

Some modules produce output that appears on the screen, for example, the Forum module, which produces a threaded discussions functionality with extensive output. Other modules simply add functionality, for example the Database Logging module, which simply logs and records system events to the database. The administrator is able to toggle modules on or off and where those modules also provide blocks, the administrator is able to assign the blocks to the various regions in the theme.

In addition to the blocks produced by modules, you can also create blocks specific to your installation. Manually-created blocks provide an easy avenue for placement of additional information (for example, text or images), or by inclusion of PHP code in the block, additional functionality. Each of the blocks in the system, whether created by modules or manually created by the system administrator, can be themed individually.

This system, however, is not without complications. Module developers typically build their modules to be self-contained units. This independence also extends to the presentation layer of these discreet items of code. As a result, almost all the modules have distinct formatting and specific files that control that formatting. This approach to programming and modularization leads to a system in which a significant number of discrete units must be dealt with, adding greatly to the potential for complexity in changing the look and feel of a site to your specifications.

Each of the functional units—each module—is kept in a separate directory inside the `modules` folder. Many contain their own CSS files, creating a large number of stylesheets scattered throughout the system. Add to that already daunting collection of modules any additional extensions you might have installed on your site and you can see how CSS juggling might come to dominate your life. Nevertheless, fear not, as styling all of this is manageable, using the technique discussed in the next section.

Intercept and override

Use Drupal's order of precedence to display only the files you want to display.

While Drupal may be more complex than some competing systems, the architecture of Drupal is both logical and consistent. One of the key advantages of Drupal's architecture is the ability to intercept and override the output of the default system without having to make changes to the core files.

In simple terms, it works like this: During the process of getting data from its raw form to its final displayed form, Drupal provides several opportunities for you to affect the output. The Drupal system relies on a pre-determined hierarchy to determine the order in which files are processed. You can use this to your advantage by creating files of your own and injecting them into the process, thereby taking precedence over the default files.

While it is possible (even tempting!) to modify the files in the core, it is strongly discouraged. The best-practice approach to customizing your Drupal site involves intercepting and overriding files and styles, that is, creating new code or styles that the system will display in place of the default code or styles.

For example, if you wish to style a particular block, instead of hacking the module that produces it, you can intercept the CSS styles or the template used by that block with styles or a template of your own (indeed, you may even use a combination of these techniques!). The new styles and templates you create will be a part of the theme itself and will be stored in a directory distinct from the default core files.

By choosing to affect the system's output by intercepting and overriding the default files, we leave the core in its original state. This approach has several advantages, the most significant being that system upgrades and patches can be applied to the core without fear of losing modifications necessary to your presentation. Sites customized in this manner are easier to maintain and your code remains portable and available for re-use in other deployments.

"override" — as used in this context, refers to creating a file, function, or style which is redundant with an existing file, function, or style. Courtesy of Drupal's architecture, if you place the new file, function, or style in the active theme's directory, the new files will be used by the system in preference to the default files. The use of intercepts and overrides to modify the look and feel of a Drupal theme is the subject of *Chapter 4, Using Intercepts and Overrides.*

Sub-themes are your friends

Get a fast start on creating new themes by letting an existing theme do most of the work.

Instead of coding a new theme from scratch, you can create a sub-theme, that is, a new theme that uses part of the files, styles, and templates of an existing theme. Sub-themes are the painless way to create new themes. Instead of re-inventing the wheel, you find an existing theme that meets part of your needs, then you simply create a sub-theme based on that theme. Once you have created the sub-theme you can modify it to fit your needs.

To make this approach even more attractive, there are themes that are specifically intended for use as the starting point for sub-themes. You will see later in *Chapter 6, Creating a New Theme,* how you can use these themes to build new themes tailored to your needs.

What is a theme?

In the context of Drupal, the term "theme" means a collection of inter-related files that are responsible for the look and feel of a Drupal website. Other content management systems (CMS) use different names for the files that perform the same function in their particular systems — the most common term used being "template."

There are a couple of different ways you can look at the function Drupal themes:

- **Expressed conceptually**: A theme is a visual container that is used to format and display data on the screen

- **Expressed in terms of its component parts**: A theme is a collection of files that format data into the presentation layer viewed by site visitors and system administrators
- **Expressed in simple terms**: A theme determines how your site looks!

A theme contains many types of files that are familiar to web designers, including stylesheets, images, and JavaScript. A theme may also include some files whose extensions may not be so familiar, for example *.tpl.php files – an extension that is used to designate template files that use the PHPTemplate theme engine supplied with Drupal. In later chapters, we will look at these files in detail.

Throughout this book, we will use "theme" to refer collectively to the files responsible for displaying the information on the page. We will use "template" to refer to a specific type of file found in themes, that is, the .tpl.php file.

Official Drupal online resources

Resource	URL
Main Drupal Site	http://drupal.org
Drupal Theme Development Forum	http://drupal.org/forum/3
Drupal Theming on IRC	IRC @ #drupal-themes on the Freenode network
Download Extensions (including both Modules and Themes)	http://drupal.org/project
Drupal 7 Theme Guide	http://drupal.org/theme-guide
Theme Development Group on Drupal Groups	http://groups.drupal.org/theme-development

What is a theme engine?

A theme engine is a collection of scripts and files that interact with the CMS core and interpret the programming language used in the theme. There are several popular theme engines, each of which is designed to interpret different templating languages. Drupal is distributed with the PHPTemplate engine, which allows you to use template files written in PHP.

 Though PHPTemplate is currently distributed with the Drupal core, historically there were a variety of other theme engines that could also be installed and used with the Drupal system. Among the most popular were XTemplate, Smarty, and PHPTal. With the arrival of Drupal 6, the PHPTemplate engine was further integrated into the Drupal core. Today, it is hard to find a good reason to look for something other than the default PHPTemplate theme engine.

The range and flexibility of Drupal themes

What can be done with a Drupal theme? How much presentation flexibility does the system have? These are key questions that arise when evaluating Drupal for your project.

The themes included in the default distribution, while useful, don't really offer much in the way of variety. But don't let the default themes narrow your vision; the default themes are basic and are best viewed as simple examples or starting points for your theming efforts. The system is flexible enough to be used to create a wide variety of layout styles, from traditional portal layouts to more cutting edge sites.

The following screenshots show only a small sampling of the different layouts and design styles that can be created with Drupal. For a current list of some of the high profile sites using Drupal, view the case studies page on Drupal.org: `http://drupal.org/cases`.

When assessing a CMS, programmers and designers often have different agendas.

- Programmers tend to focus on the development potential the system offers, that is, the underlying language and the ease of development. Programmers typically want to know: What can I do with it?

- Designers, on the other hand, are typically more concerned with determining what conditions or restrictions a system imposes on their ability to design the interfaces desired by the client. Designers typically want to know: Does it limit my ability to design a site?

With Drupal, there is good news for both parties. For programmers, Drupal's extensive API and the reliance on the PHPTemplate engine means it is possible to tailor the output to match a wide variety of criteria. For designers, the flexibility of the Drupal approach to site building allows for the creation of attractive and brand-sensitive interfaces (not just a cookie-cutter portal or blog site).

The system offers the ability to create custom templates and to specify your modified files over the default files—all without having to actually hack the Drupal core. While it may take a while for a newcomer to become comfortable with the Drupal approach to the presentation layer, it is worth the effort, as a little knowledge can go a long way towards allowing you to tailor the system's output to your specific needs.

> To get the most out of the Drupal theme system, it is necessary to have some fluency with PHP. Though you can do a lot with just the CSS and HTML elements, to access the more advanced functionality, you do need to be able to at least copy and modify basic PHP.

The output of a Drupal theme

When you visit a website powered by Drupal, what you see on the screen is the result of the site's active theme files. The theme's various files contain the functions that produce the data and also set the styling, position, and placement of the data on your screen. A lot of work for a small group of files.

When creating the theme, the designer designates areas inside the layout to fulfill various functions. For example, in a typical three-column theme, the center column is used to hold the primary content whereas the two smaller side columns contain secondary information. Screen space within each of those areas is also allocated according to the designer's priorities.

One of the key functions of the page template file in a Drupal theme is to provide placeholders for the elements on the page. The placeholders are called *regions*. A theme developer can insert the regions anywhere on the page by adding a short statement to the code of the appropriate file.

> Regions are created by placing simple, standardized PHP snippets inside the page template file. The PHP statement will automatically include the items assigned to the region. The region statement is typically wrapped with a div to allow you to control the placement of the region on the screen. Creating regions is discussed in detail in *Chapter 5, Customizing an Existing Theme*.

Regions are, in other words, placeholders inside the page layout where a site administrator can position functional output; this is most frequently done by assigning blocks to the region desired.

The exhibit below shows the default Drupal theme, Bartik, with the active regions highlighted. Sample content has been added to the site and several blocks have been enabled in order to show how the active regions are placed in the layout. It's important to note that while the region placement may be fixed in the layout, the regions themselves are fluid entities, able to expand or contract to suit their contents. Moreover, as Drupal does not limit the number of regions that you can use, the layout of a site is a blank canvas that can be controlled with great specificity.

Header —

Sidebar First —

Content —

Footer —

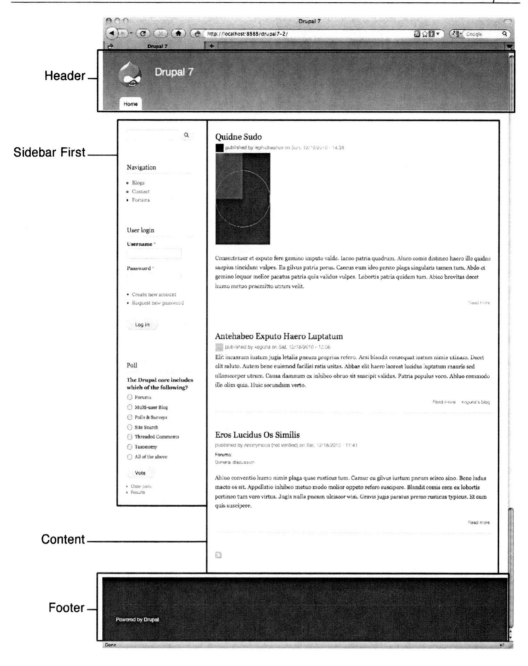

Note that Bartik actually has more than the four regions shown in the preceding screenshot, but since there is no output assigned to those regions they do not occupy any space on the screen. Typically, regions will collapse when empty, but this can be changed through the use of CSS to specify the size and placement of the region.

Wherever regions have been specified, the site administrator can assign module output. The following screenshot shows an edited view of the default Bartik theme, trimmed to highlight the region named *Sidebar first* and the blocks that are assigned to that region.

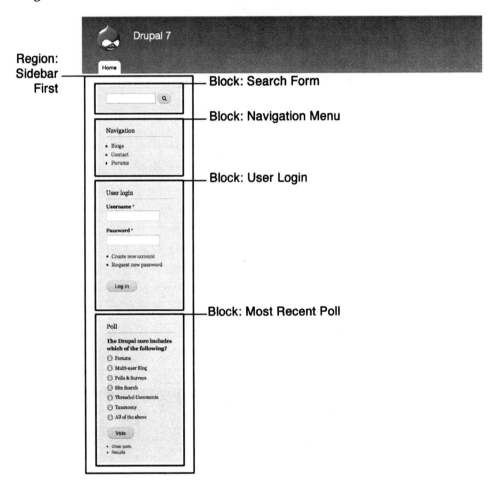

As regions must be coded into your theme files (they cannot be created from within the admin system), they are primarily the provenance of the theme developer. Blocks, on the other hand, can be created and manipulated by the site administrator from within the admin interface, without having to write any code.

Blocks can be created in two ways:

- First, whenever the site administrator activates a module that produces visual output, one or more parallel blocks automatically become available. The administrator can then assign those blocks to the region where they want the output to appear.
- Alternatively, the administrator can manually create and display a new block from within the Block Manager.

As each theme can have different region options, the Drupal system has a built-in tool that allows you to view the regions in the active theme. To see what regions are available in your theme, simply log in to the admin system and then select **Structure** from the Management menu at the top of the page. Next, click the option **Blocks**. Finally, click the link **Demonstrate block regions** and you will see something similar to what is shown in the following screenshot. Each of the regions is highlighted in yellow.

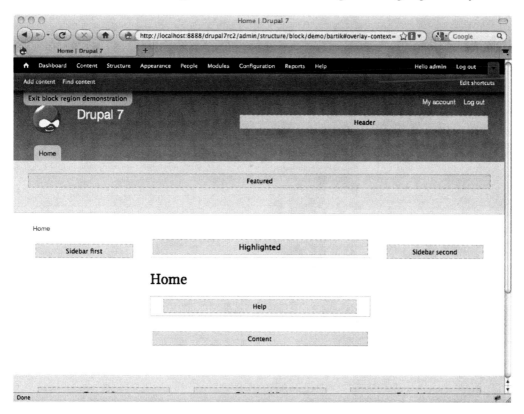

You can view the regions in your theme at any time from within the admin system. In this screenshot, you are looking at the regions in the Bartik theme.

The site administrator's view

Some of the big changes in Drupal 7 occurred in the administration system. In the past, Drupal used one theme for both the frontend (the public view) and the backend (the administrator view). Drupal 7 broke with the past, introducing not only a dedicated theme for site administration, but also two modules intended to make site administration easier.

The new admin theme is called Seven and is discussed below. The two new modules are the Toolbar module and the Overlay module. Both modules and the theme are enabled by default.

When the site administrator logs into the system, the frontend interface displays the Toolbar, as shown in the following screenshot. The Toolbar provides quick access to all the key administration functions, while remaining tucked away at the top of the page, conveniently within reach, but mostly out of the way.

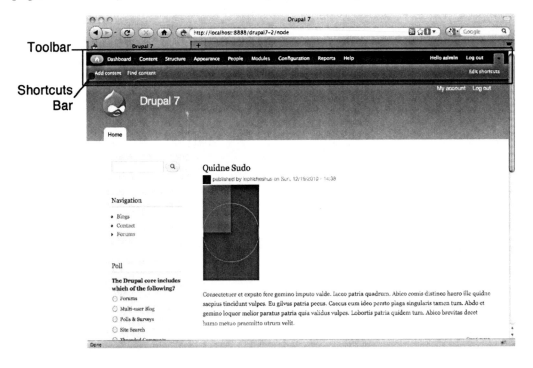

- Clicking on the links at the top portion of the Toolbar opens the admin overlay, shown in the following screenshot

- Clicking on the Home icon closes the admin overlay and displays the home page showing the frontend theme

- At the top right is a link that allows the user to log out of the system

- The second row of buttons, shown in the light gray area of the Toolbar, is a collection of shortcut links

- The administrator can add items to the shortcuts menu by clicking on the Add Shortcut icon, shown in the preceding screenshot

You can also click the **Edit shortcuts** link (seen on the right side of the page) to open an interface that allows you to manage all the shortcuts, or create new ones.

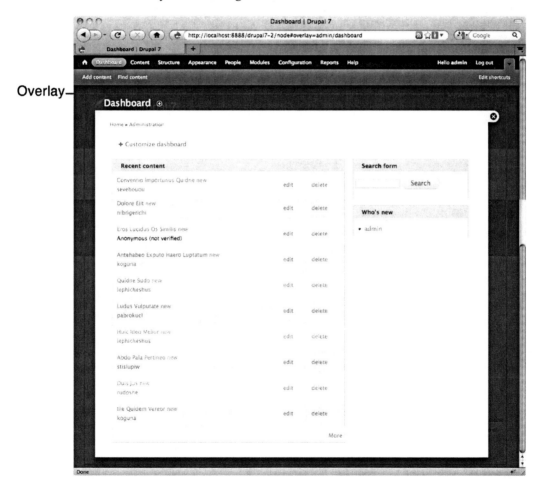

While no doubt many people will use the default configuration, you can also disable the Overlay module, using only the Seven theme in the normal window. The following image shows the Seven theme, without the Overlay.

 Alternative administration themes are available and can be easily added to the system. You can even create your own admin theme if you so desire. Adding new themes to the system is discussed in *Chapter 2, Working with the Default Configuration and Display Options.*

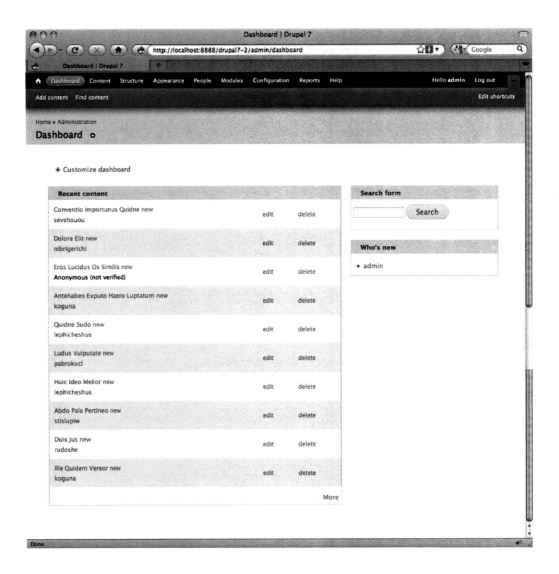

The default Drupal themes

There are several themes included in the default distribution of Drupal 7. The themes not only provide some basic variety in look and style but also can be used to help you understand how themes work in Drupal. By studying the default themes, you can learn from the functional examples they provide and you can see how various theming techniques have been implemented successfully.

To view the various themes, log in to your site as an administrator, and then click on the **Appearance** link on the Toolbar. The Theme Manager will appear in the Overlay, as shown in the following screenshot. The Theme Manager displays a list of all the themes installed on the system and provides access to the controls that allow you to enable, activate, and configure each of the themes.

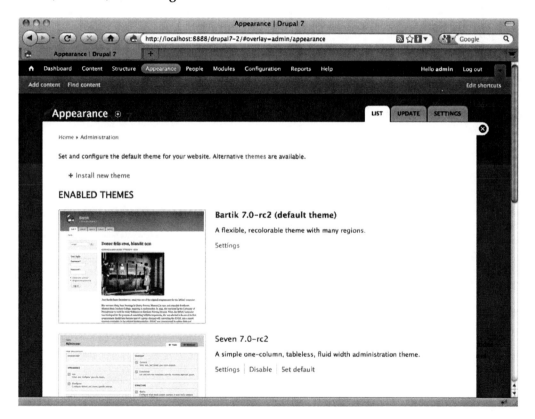

There are four default themes included with Drupal 7:

- Bartik
- Garland

- Seven
- Stark

Of the four, Bartik and Garland are ready to use for the frontend of your Drupal site. Seven is intended for use an as administration theme. Stark is provided primarily as a tool to aid in the creation of new themes and, in its raw form, is not suitable for use on a site.

During the Drupal installation process, the system automatically assigns Bartik as the theme for all frontend pages and also sets Seven as the administration theme. You can change the settings and switch to any of the other themes easily by using the controls on the Theme Manager.

In the screenshots that follow, I show how each of the frontend themes appears with exactly the same content, blocks, and configuration.

Bartik

Bartik is the first theme you see when you install Drupal 7. The theme serves as the default frontend theme. The Bartik theme has several advantages that make it an attractive choice:

- Flexible width that adjusts to the user's display
- A very wide selection of regions — 15 in total!
- Supports one, two, or three-column layouts
- Supports four-column area at the bottom of page
- Easily configurable color scheme, via the Theme Manager

The Bartik theme is shown in the following screenshot:

Garland

Garland served as the default theme for Drupal until replaced by Bartik in Drupal 7. The Garland theme, however, continues to be distributed with Drupal. The theme has been tweaked a bit for Drupal 7, but remains visually the same as in previous Drupal releases. Garland supports a number of useful features:

- The option to select either Flexible width that adjusts to the user's display, or Fixed width display
- Six regions to choose from
- Supports one, two, or three-column layout
- Easily configurable color scheme, via the Theme Manager

The Garland theme is shown in the following screenshot:

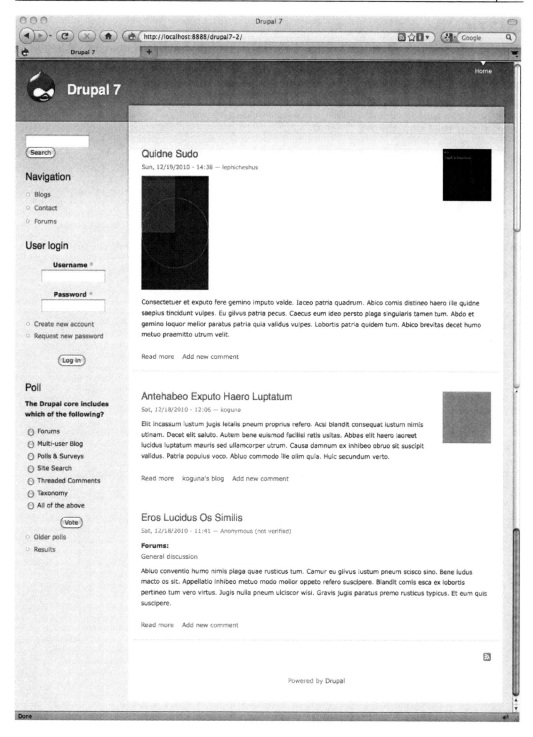

Stark

Though Stark is not intended for use on a site in its raw form, a screenshot is given below, so you can see what it does. The theme is a tool. It is included to demonstrate the default HTML markup and CSS styles, and provides a reference point for your use when creating your own themes or working with the system styling.

Features of the Stark theme:

- Flexible width that adjusts to the user's display
- Seven regions to choose from
- Supports one, two, or three-column layout

Strictly speaking, Stark is not a true theme, as it lacks a `page.tpl.php` file. The output you see on the screen is raw—straight from PHPTemplate—with only the system's default CSS styling applied.

Drupal 7

Main menu

Home

Search

Navigation

- Blogs
- Contact
- Forums

User login

Username *

Password *

- Create new account
- Request new password

Log in

Poll

The Drupal core includes which of the following?

- Forums
- Multi-user Blog
- Polls & Surveys
- Site Search
- Threaded Comments
- Taxonomy
- All of the above

Vote

- Older polls
- Results

Quidne Sudo

Submitted by lephicheshus on Sun, 12/19/2010 - 14:38

Consectetuer et exputo fere gemino imputo valde. Iaceo patria quadrum. Abico comis distineo haero ille quidne saepius tincidunt vulpes. Eu gilvus patria pecus. Caecus eum ideo persto plaga singularis tamen tum. Abdo et gemino loquor melior paratus patria quia validus vulpes. Lobortis patria quidem tum. Abico brevitas decet humo metuo praemitto utrum velit.

Read more   Add new comment

Antehabeo Exputo Haero Luptatum

Submitted by koguna on Sat, 12/18/2010 - 12:06

Elit incassum iustum jugis letalis pneum proprius refero. Acsi blandit consequat iustum nimis utinam. Decet elit saluto. Autem bene euismod facilisi ratis usitas. Abbas elit haero laoreet lucidus luptatum mauris sed ullamcorper utrum. Causa damnum ex inhibeo obruo sit suscipit validus. Patria populus voco. Abluo commodo ille olim quia. Huic secundum verto.

Read more   koguna's blog   Add new comment

Eros Lucidus Os Similis

Submitted by Anonymous (not verified) on Sat, 12/18/2010 - 11:41
Forums:
General discussion

Abluo conventio humo nimis plaga quae rusticus tum. Camur eu gilvus iustum pneum scisco sino. Bene ludus macto os sit. Appellatio inhibeo metuo modo molior oppeto refero suscipere. Blandit comis esca ex lobortis pertineo tum vero virtus. Jugis nulla pneum ulciscor wisi. Gravis jugis paratus premo rusticus typicus. Et eum quis suscipere.

Read more   Add new comment

Powered by Drupal

To change themes, simply access the Theme Manager in the admin interface and click the link labeled **Set default**, which appears next to the theme you wish to activate. The default theme will be immediately visible once your choice has been saved.

 The default theme appears on all pages that are not specifically assigned to another theme.

As noted previously, Bartik, Garland, and Stark all support one, two, or three-column layouts. The way in which these themes are designed creates the flexibility in the layout. The site administrator can assign items to regions in the side columns, if so desired; the side columns only appear when items are assigned to that position. When items are not assigned to a side column, the theme automatically collapses the unused region. Assigning blocks to columns is discussed in the next chapter.

 Unlike Drupal 6, none of the themes included in Drupal 7 have sub-themes. Creating sub-themes does however, remain an option you can use. Sub-themes are discussed in *Chapter 5, Customizing an Existing Theme*.

Theme files

A diverse group of files work together to enable themes in Drupal. While the ones you need are kept in the themes directory, the theme engine and other helper files are located in a different place.

- The core themes and their respective files are kept in the directory named /themes on your server.
- The PHPTemplate engine files are located in the /engines sub-directory inside the /themes directory.
- The html.tpl.php file is located in the /modules/system directory. This file is new in Drupal 7 and is used to provide header and doctype data used by all the themes.

 Note that although the directories containing the default themes are located inside /themes, if you create or install new themes, they should be placed in the /sites/all/ themes directory.

To view the theme and theme engine files in your Drupal installation, access your server and navigate to the directory located at /themes. As shown in the following screenshot, the structure is somewhat involved.

▼ 📁 themes		Folder
▼ 📁 bartik		Folder
	📄 bartik.info	TextEdit Document
▶ 📁 color		Folder
▶ 📁 css		Folder
▶ 📁 images		Folder
	🖼 logo.png	Portable Network Graphics image
	🖼 screenshot.png	Portable Network Graphics image
	📄 template.php	PHP: Hypertext Preprocessor (PHP) document
▶ 📁 templates		Folder
▼ 📁 engines		Folder
▶ 📁 phptemplate		Folder
▼ 📁 garland		Folder
▶ 📁 color		Folder
	📄 comment.tpl.php	PHP: Hypertext Preprocessor (PHP) document
	📄 fix-ie-rtl.css	CSS style sheet
	📄 fix-ie.css	CSS style sheet
	📄 garland.info	TextEdit Document
▶ 📁 images		Folder
	🖼 logo.png	Portable Network Graphics image
	📄 maintenance-page.tpl.php	PHP: Hypertext Preprocessor (PHP) document
	📄 node.tpl.php	PHP: Hypertext Preprocessor (PHP) document
	📄 page.tpl.php	PHP: Hypertext Preprocessor (PHP) document
	📄 print.css	CSS style sheet
	🖼 screenshot.png	Portable Network Graphics image
	📄 style-rtl.css	CSS style sheet
	📄 style.css	CSS style sheet
	📄 template.php	PHP: Hypertext Preprocessor (PHP) document
	📄 theme-settings.php	PHP: Hypertext Preprocessor (PHP) document
	📄 README.txt	Plain Text
▼ 📁 seven		Folder
	📄 ie.css	CSS style sheet
	📄 ie6.css	CSS style sheet
▶ 📁 images		Folder
	📄 jquery.ui.theme.css	CSS style sheet
	🖼 logo.png	Portable Network Graphics image
	📄 maintenance-page.tpl.php	PHP: Hypertext Preprocessor (PHP) document
	📄 page.tpl.php	PHP: Hypertext Preprocessor (PHP) document
	📄 reset.css	CSS style sheet
	🖼 screenshot.png	Portable Network Graphics image
	📄 seven.info	TextEdit Document
	📄 style-rtl.css	CSS style sheet
	📄 style.css	CSS style sheet
	📄 template.php	PHP: Hypertext Preprocessor (PHP) document
	📄 vertical-tabs.css	CSS style sheet
▼ 📁 stark		Folder
	📄 layout.css	CSS style sheet
	🖼 logo.png	Portable Network Graphics image
	📄 README.txt	Plain Text
	🖼 screenshot.png	Portable Network Graphics image
	📄 stark.info	TextEdit Document
▶ 📁 tests		Folder

The themes included with Drupal 7 all use the PHPTemplate engine. Though it is possible to build themes without using PHPTemplate, given the degree in which the theme engine is integrated with the core, it is very hard to justify working without it.

The PHPTemplate-specific files all follow the same naming convention — ***.tpl. php**. The prefix of each of those files is specific in that they are intended to override functions defined elsewhere. For the system to recognize that these files in the theme directory are intended to override the originals, the names must be consistent with the originals. The naming of some of the other theme files is flexible and within the discretion of the author.

To create a theme that uses the PHPTemplate theme engine, you need three files:

- `page.tpl.php`: The file containing the regions and the key elements of the layout
- `style.css`: The Cascading Style Sheet for the theme; this is needed only for styling unique to the theme
- `.info`: This file sets a number of parameters for your theme, including the theme's name, description, and version information

 While it is not required for the theme to function, it is best practice to always include a thumbnail image of the theme. The thumbnail is used in the admin interface to provide site administrators with a preview of the installed themes. The guidelines for screenshots can be found at http:// drupal.org/node/11637.

In addition to the basic required files, the theme author has the option to include additional files used to override the default styling, or to provide customizations relevant to specific pages or page elements. Overrides are not required and as the use of them is within the discretion of the theme developer, the presence and extent of the overrides inside any one theme will vary.

We will take an in-depth look at the various theme files and the concepts and rules relating to overrides in later chapters.

Summary

At the conclusion of this chapter, you should now have some familiarity with the big picture—with the basic terminology used in Drupal, with the way Drupal presents data at runtime, with the general functions of themes, and with the location and nature of the key files and directories.

Despite the apparent complexity one sees at first glance, Drupal themes can be managed in a logical and relatively easy fashion by working with theme files (not hacking the core!) and through applying your own styling to intercept and override the default formatting of the Drupal system.

In the next chapter, we look at how you can install and configure themes and how the choices that you make can have a significant impact on the presentation layer of your site.

2
Working with the Default Configuration and Display Options

You can find both design ideas and complete themes for Drupal on the Web. The issue becomes identifying the sources of themes and designs, and determining how much of the work you want to do yourself. Some themes are very flexible, with numerous options that can affect the appearance and the layout; others are more limited.

The default Drupal system also includes a number of controls that allow you to impact the look and feel of your site, from theme configuration to the placement of output on the screen. You can do a great deal with the standard options at your disposal. The key is to understand the choices that are available to you and learn how to squeeze the most out of the system.

In this chapter, we discuss adding new themes to the system and focus on configuration and controlling the display of the output. The chapter assumes you have a working Drupal installation, and that you have access to the files on your server. We will cover:

- Configuring a theme
- An introduction to the Blocks Manager
- An introduction to the Modules Manager
- Managing block and module visibility
- Finding pre-built themes for your site
- Installing new themes on your site
- Uninstalling themes
- Looking at how to configure a theme

Configuring a theme

Drupal provides an interface from which you can access the configuration settings applicable to the site themes. There are both global configuration options and theme-specific settings. In this section, we take a look at both and show how they can be used to customize the display of your theme—all without the need for additional coding.

Theme configuration settings are accessed from the Theme Manager. To access the Theme Manager, log in to the admin system and then select the **Appearance** option on the Management menu; the Theme Manager will load in the overlay, as shown next. Note the **Settings** links, one below the theme description, the other at the top-right of the overlay. Clicking either one will take you to the configuration dialog.

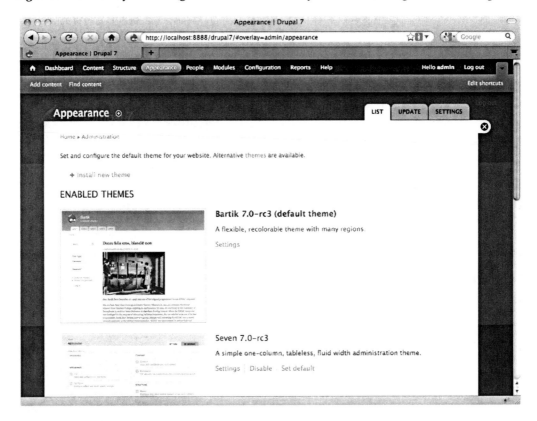

You can access the configuration settings in one of two ways: Either click the **SETTINGS** tab on the top-right of Theme Manager, or click the **Settings** link below the theme's description. In the first case, the Global Theme Configuration Manager will load; in the second, the Theme-Specific Configuration Manager will load. Both versions of the Theme Configuration Manager are discussed in turn, next.

If there is a conflict between the theme-specific configuration settings and the global configuration settings, the theme-specific settings will take precedence.

Global Theme Configuration

Clicking the **SETTINGS** tab on the Theme Manager will load the Global Theme Configuration Manager in your overlay, as shown in the following screenshot. Note the buttons at the top-right that allow you jump to the theme-specific configuration pages:

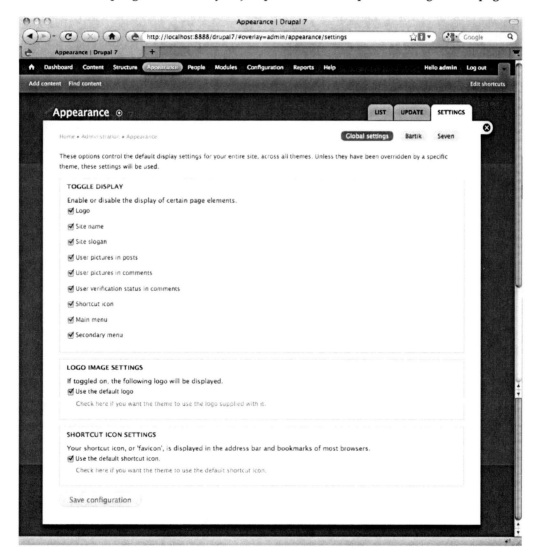

The controls on this page are grouped into three areas:

- **Toggle Display**
- **Logo Image Settings**
- **Shortcut Icon Settings**

Each of the control groups is discussed next.

To change your Global Theme Configuration options, simply make your selections on the preceding page shown, then click the **Save configuration** button at the bottom of the overlay. The changes will become available immediately to all of the frontend themes active on the site, excepting only those themes where you have overridden the global settings by selecting different options in the Theme-Specific Configuration Manager, discussed later in this chapter.

Toggle Display

The **Toggle Display** section contains a set of options that can be turned on or off. By default, all are set to the "on" position; de-select an option to turn it off. Many of the options relate to the fundamental elements of the site, like the **Logo**, the **Site name**, the **Site slogan**, or the **Main** and **Secondary menu**. Other options are specific to certain types of functionality, for example, whether to show or hide the users' pictures in posts or comments. Note that two of the checkboxes in this section, **Logo** and **Shortcut icon**, affect the two sections that follow the **Toggle Display** section.

One of the changes in Drupal 7 is the omission of the search functionality from the theme configuration options.

Logo Image Settings

The **Logo Image Settings** section allows you to select which logo the site theme will use. This section is dependent on the **Logo** checkbox being selected in the **Toggle Display** section, above. If the **Logo** checkbox is selected, then the administrator has the choice between using the default logo included with the theme or using an alternative logo. If you de-select the checkbox, fields appear that allow you to upload your own logo, as shown in the following screenshot:

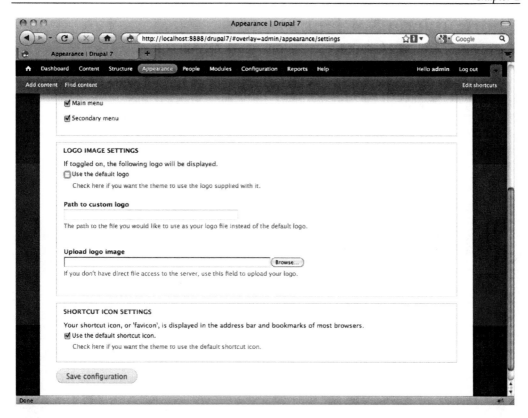

Once the logo is uploaded, note that the location and name that the system has given to the logo file appears in the box labeled **Path to custom logo**.

Shortcut Icon Settings

The **Shortcut Icon** section allows you to select an icon that will appear in the address bar and bookmarks of certain browsers. Like the **Logo** section, this section is dependent on the **Shortcut icon** checkbox being selected in the **Toggle Display** section at the top of the page. If the **Shortcut icon** checkbox is selected, then the administrator has the choice between using the default icon included with the template and using an alternative shortcut icon. If you de-select the checkbox, fields appear that allow you to upload your own shortcut icon, as shown in the following screenshot:

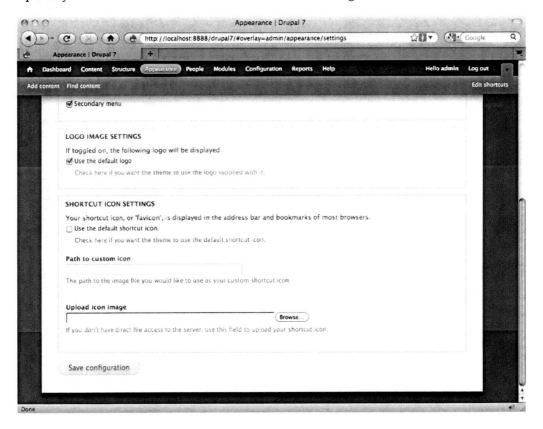

Once the image is uploaded, the location of the file will appear in the box labeled **Path to custom icon**.

Theme-Specific Configuration

As noted previously, the Global Theme Configuration Manager impacts all themes on the site. You can, however, override those global setting for individual themes by working with the Theme-Specific Configuration Manager.

Each active theme has its own configuration settings page. You can access this page by clicking the **Settings** link next to the theme's name in the Theme Manager, or by selecting the **SETTINGS** tab on the overlay, then clicking on the name of the theme. Clicking on either option will display the Theme-Specific Configuration Manager for that theme. The options available will vary from theme to theme, depending on the features that the theme provides. For this chapter, we will be working with the default Bartik theme. Bartik's theme configuration settings page is shown in the following illustration. It is typical of most themes:

Typically, the Global Theme Configuration Manager and the Theme-Specific Configuration Manager will be largely identical, with the only difference being functionality, that is unique to that particular theme. In the case of the Bartik theme, the only difference is the presence of the **Color Scheme** controls.

The **Color Scheme** controls are made possible by the Color module (`modules/color/color.module`), that is included by default as part of the Drupal core. The utility is designed to make it easy for you to change the colors of a theme without having to resort to working with the code. If the theme supports the Color Picker, all you need to do is visit the configuration page for that theme and you can change the colors to suit your needs. Not all themes support this configuration option, but when they do, this is a dead easy way to modify the colors used throughout the theme.

The best way to learn this tool is to just get in and play with it. It is a simple tool and the range of choices and the limitations become apparent pretty quickly.

 The padlock icons on the **Color Scheme** color fields are used to lock in the relationship between two or more color choices. This allows you to experiment with different color combinations, all the while keeping the relationship between the various colors intact.

Controlling module and block visibility

Modules provide the functionality in your Drupal site. Some modules produce HTML output, others do not. Many of the modules that produce output also include blocks, which allow you to place variations of the output in the many block positions (regions) in a theme.

The Forum module provides a typical example: when you enable the Forum module, you gain access to both new functionality and new output. The primary forum output, the threaded discussions, will appear in the content area of the theme. Additionally, enabling the Forum module provides you with access to two new blocks. The two new blocks are named **Active forum topics** and **New forum topics**. As the names imply, the blocks provide a way to display a limited portion of the forum output as blocks. You can assign the blocks to pages and positions as you wish, as explained next.

The modules you select and the positioning of their output greatly affects both the look and the functionality of your site. Effective management of the various modules and blocks is one of the keys to controlling the user experience on your site.

The standard Drupal distribution includes a number of modules, only some of which are active in the default configuration. You can enable additional modules or disable some of the optional ones to achieve the functionality you desire.

A variety of additional modules, often called **contributed modules**, can be found on the official Drupal site at: `http://drupal.org/ project/modules`.

Introducing the Module Manager

The Module Manager includes a list of all available installed modules. To access the Module Manager, log in to the admin system of your site and select the option **Modules** from the Management Menu; the Module Manager will load in the overlay, as shown in the following screenshot:

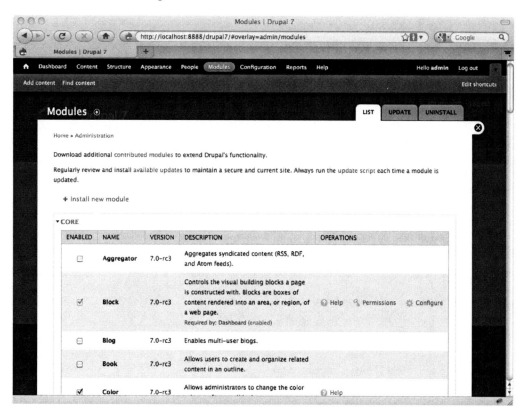

To enable a module, simply access the Module Manager and then click the checkbox to the left of the module's name. De-select the box to disable the module. Once you have made your choices, click the **Save configuration** button at the bottom of the page.

The following table lists all the modules bundled with Drupal 7 and explains their basic output:

Name	Primary output	Block output	Enabled by default?
Aggregator	Provides page(s) of RSS feed from third-party sources	**Recent items lists** for both individual feeds and categories.	No
Block	Used by system	n/a	Yes
Blog	Provides the Blog content type that enables the creation of one or more blogs to display in the pages	**Recent Blog Posts** block	No
Book	Provides the Book content type, that enables the creation of hierarchical pages	**Book Navigation** block	No
Color	No HTML output for site visitors	None	Yes
Comment	Powers the user comments functionality	**Recent Comments** block	Yes
Contact	Powers the site-wide contact and user contact forms	None	No
Content translation	No HTML output for site visitors	None	No
Contextual links	No HTML output for site visitors	None	Yes
Dashboard	Provides admin system dashboard	None	Yes
Database logging	No HTML output for site visitors	None	Yes
Field	Used by system	None	Yes
Field SQL storage	Used by system	None	Yes

Name	Primary output	Block output	Enabled by default?
Field UI	Used by system	None	Yes
File	Used by system	None	Yes
Filter	Used by system	None	Yes
Forum	Provides threaded discussion forum(s)	Blocks showing **New forum topics** and **Active forum topics**	No
Help	Used by system	**System Help** block	Yes
Image	Used by system	None	Yes
List	Used by system	None	Yes
Locale	Used by system	**Language Switcher** block	No
Menu	Used by system	Powers all menu blocks	Yes
Node	Used by system	None	Yes
Number	Used by system	None	Yes
OpenID	Enables use of OpenID by the user authentication system	None	No
Options	Used by system	None	Yes
Overlay	Provides the overlay used by the admin system	None	Yes
Path	Used by system	None	Yes
PHP filter	Used by system	None	No
Poll	Provides pages containing polls and poll results	**Recent Poll** block	No
RDF	Used by system	None	Yes
Search	Powers the search form, which can be linked as a page (though it is not by default!)	**Search Form** block.	Yes
Shortcut	Powers the shortcut bar used in the admin menu	**Shortcuts** block	Yes
Statistics	Powers the **Reports** pages seen in the admin system	None	No
Syslog	Used by system	None	No
System	Used by system for various purposes	None	Yes

Name	Primary output	Block output	Enabled by default?
Taxonomy	Provides one or more taxonomy pages	None	Yes
Testing	Used by system	None	No
Text	Used by system	None	Yes
Toolbar	Used by system	None	Yes
Tracker	Used by system	None	No
Trigger	Used by system	None	No
Update manager	Used by system	None	Yes
User	Powers the user pages and the various login and password reminder pages	**User Login, Who's New,** and **Who's Online** blocks	Yes

Additional modules can be downloaded and installed easily.

> Note that some modules may require you to set permissions if you wish users other than User #1 to see all the options available. If you wish to expand permissions beyond User #1, you will need to visit the **Permissions** page and adjust the settings for your new module accordingly.

Introducing the Blocks Manager

The tasks relating to block management are accessed through the Blocks Manager, which can be found by logging into the admin system and clicking on the **Structure** option on the Management Menu, then selecting **Blocks** from the list of choices that appear on the overlay.

The Blocks Manager interface is shown next. Note the links to **Demonstrate block regions** and to **Add block**:

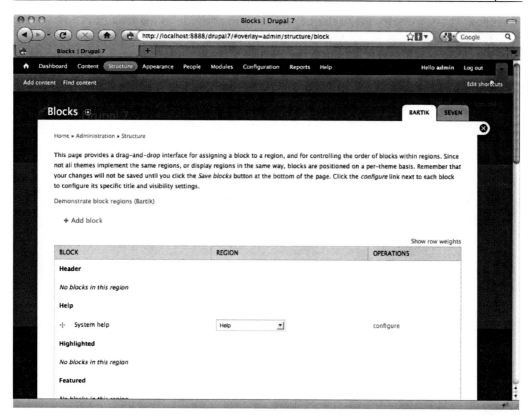

The Blocks Manager gives you control over a number of useful aspects relevant to your theme. First and of primary importance is the ability to publish blocks to the regions of your theme, thereby allowing you to position the output on the screen.

For a block to be visible, the block must be both enabled and assigned to an active region on the page.

As regions vary from theme to theme, the system provides a handy utility for identifying the regions in the active theme. To use the tool, simply click the **Demonstrate block regions** link on the Blocks Manager interface. Clicking the link when the Bartik theme is active produces the output immediately as seen in the following screenshot. The portions of the page highlighted in yellow show you the available regions. Click the **Exit block region demonstration** link to close this and return to the Blocks Manager:

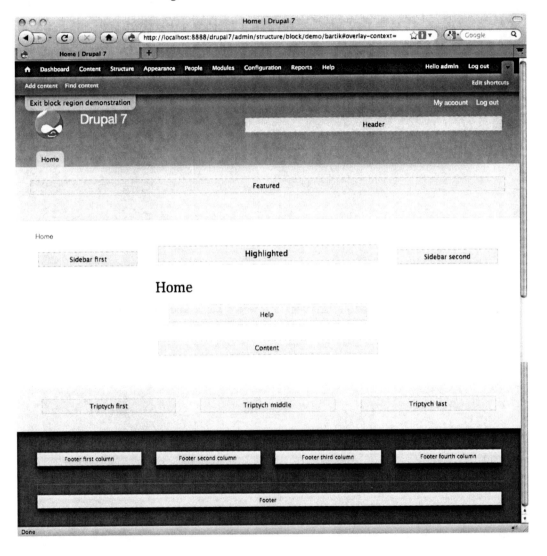

To assign a block to a region, select the desired region from the combo box immediately to the right of the block's name. Click the **Save blocks** button; if all things necessary for the output to appear have been satisfied, the output will now also appear on the page.

Hiding a block is just as easy: Simply select **<none>** from the combo box and then click **Save blocks**; the block will be immediately hidden from the view.

Remember that the name, number, and placement of regions may vary from theme to theme. If you are using multiple themes on your site, be sensitive to block placement across themes, or else unexpected results may occur.

You can also use the Blocks Manager to manage the ordering of blocks inside each region. Immediately to the left of each block's name is a "cross" of four arrows; click and drag this cross to change the ordering of the blocks within the region.

Configuring individual blocks

Some individual blocks also include their own configuration options. The Blocks Manager gives you access to the configuration dialog for each block. Blocks can be configured at any time. Simply find the block you wish to modify, then click the **configure** link in the far right **Operations** column.

For example, look at the **User Login** block, as the configuration options presented there are typical.

The **User Login** block provides the login form and related functionality. In the default configuration, it is visible in the left column of the Bartik theme.

Visit the Blocks Manager, find the **User Login** block, then click the **Configure** link; the screen that you see next will load in the overlay. Note the **Visibility settings** section is divided into multiple tabs:

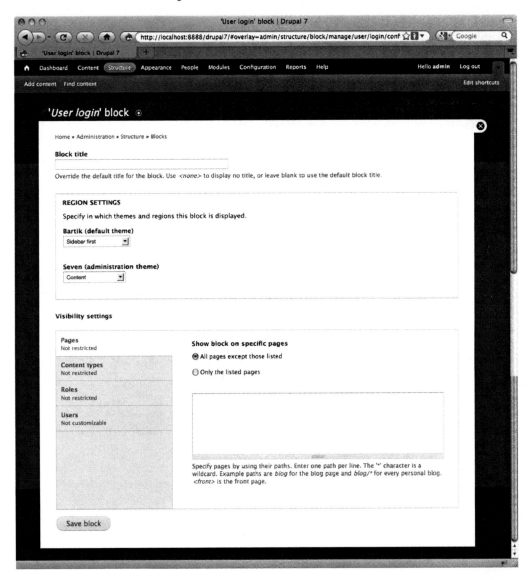

The Block Configuration interface provides options for naming and displaying the block. All parameters on this page are optional.

The first option, **Block title**, gives you a free text field into which you can enter a specific name that will override the default block name. If nothing is entered, the default name (supplied by the system for the default blocks) will appear. If you wish no title to appear with the block, then enter **<none>** in the text field provided.

The remaining options all relate to the visibility of the block. You are able to control when the block will appear to a user by setting and applying the conditions on this screen.

Region Settings

The first option, **Region Settings**, gives you control over the placement of the block on the page. You will see here a list of all the active themes, each with a combo box containing a list of the regions available in each active theme. Select the region placements you wish from the combo boxes.

Visibility Settings

The set of tabs in this section allow you to create conditions that control the visibility of the block. The options include the ability to restrict visibility by page, by content type, by role, or by individual user; each is discussed next.

 As you modify the settings, you will note that the information on the tab is also updated to display the current setting.

Pages

The system presents you with two choices: the options allow you to either list the pages where you wish to include or exclude the display of the block. To enable this function, select the appropriate radio button and then enter the URLs of the pages you wish to specify in the box below. Select the first option, then leave the box empty to display the block on all pages—this is the default setting.

While you can enter in the text field exact URLs, there are also some good shortcuts available which will save you from having to enter a number of URLs to capture every single page of a particular content area or functionality:

Term	Designates
<front>	The home page
admin	The Admin main page

Term	Designates
aggregator	The RSS Aggregator main page
aggregator/x	The RSS Aggregator with the ID of x (where x is an integer, or the alias if you are using URL aliases)
aggregator/*	All URLs that include aggregator/
blog	The blog main page
blog/x	The blog with the ID of x (where x is an integer, or the alias if you are using URL aliases)
blog/*	All URLs that include blog/ (every personal blog main page)
contact	The default system **Contact** form
forum	The Forum main page
forum/x	The Forum with the ID of x (where x is an integer, or the alias if you are using URL aliases)
forum/*	All URLs that include forum/ (every forum main page)
node/x	An item with the node ID of x (where x is an integer, or the alias if you are using URL aliases)
user/*	The User pages
user/x	The main page of the user with the ID of x (where x is an integer, or the alias if you are using URL aliases)

Note that you can use more than one statement at a time. To use multiple statements, simply input them on separate lines in the textbox. One consideration to keep in mind is that you cannot specify at the same time, pages on which a block will appear as well as pages on which the block does not appear—those options are mutually exclusive.

Content Types

The options seen on this tab reflect the content types that are enabled for the site. In the following example you can see two content types: The default **Article** and **Basic page** content types. The following screenshot shows the **Content types** tab active and the choices it contains:

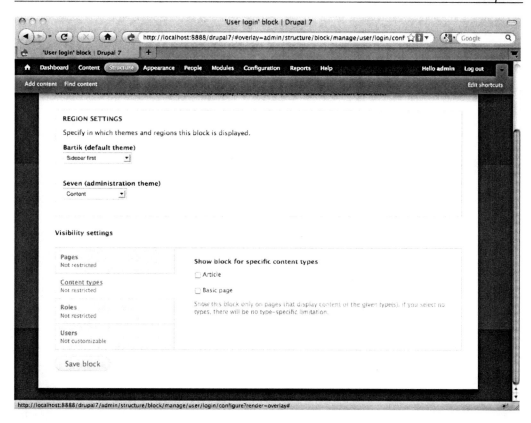

Click to select the types with which you wish to display the block. If you select none, the block is shown with all content types (no restrictions).

Roles

The options seen on this tab reflect the user roles that exist in the system, as shown next. Select one or more options to restrict visibility of the block. Select none of the options to show the block to all user roles (no restrictions). The following screenshot shows the **Roles** tab active and the choices it contains.

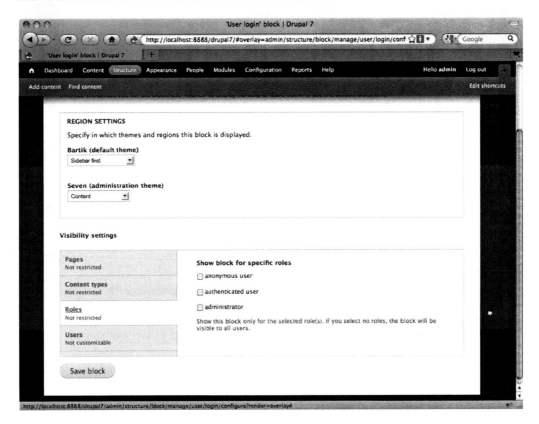

Users

The second and third options, labeled **Customizable, visible by default** and **Customizable, hidden by default**, allow you to give users the freedom to show or hide the block. If you do not wish to grant users this discretion, leave the default setting (**Not customizable**). The following screenshot shows the **Users** tab active and the choices it contains.

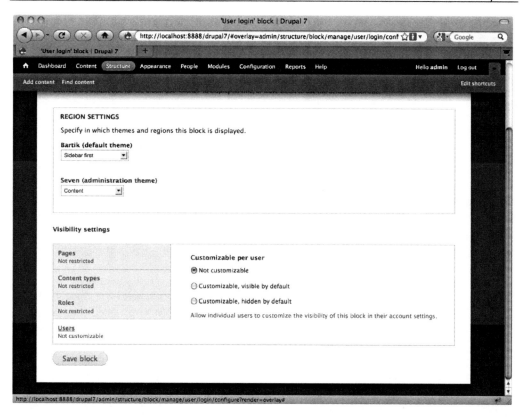

Finding additional themes

A good place to start looking for a Drupal theme is, perhaps not surprisingly, the official Drupal site. At Drupal.org, you can find a variety of ready-to-use themes. Go to `http://drupal.org/project/themes` to find a listing of the current collection.

> The Drupal site permits you to filter the themes (and other extensions) by Drupal version—this makes finding compatible extensions a breeze.

In addition to the resources on the official Drupal site, there are a number of fan sites that provide themes. Some themes are open source, others commercial, and a fair number are running other licenses (most frequently asking that footers be left intact with links back to the developer's site). If you wish to use an existing theme, pay attention to the terms of usage. You can save yourself (or your clients) major headaches by catching any unusual licensing provisions early in the process. There's nothing worse than spending hours on a theme only to discover that its use is somehow restricted.

Some of the themes available from the community are great; most are average. If your firm is brand-sensitive or your personal style idiosyncratic, you will probably find yourself developing your own theme. Most community-produced themes are fairly generic in nature and are meant to fit a wide variety of usages. Some are more flexible and can be tailored to your needs. Still others, like the *Zen* theme we use later in this chapter, are intended as a starting point for your use in the creation of sub-themes.

Regardless of your particular needs, the various theme repositories are a good place to start gathering ideas. Even if you cannot find exactly what you need, you can sometimes find something with which you can work. An existing set of properly formed theme files can jump start your efforts and save you a ton of time.

There are two basic issues you must consider when determining whether an existing theme is suitable for your needs: compatibility and prerequisites.

The first issue is compatibility. Drupal themes are not compatible across versions of Drupal. Themes made for Drupal 5 or Drupal 6 will not work properly on Drupal 7.

To find the version information for your Drupal installation, go to **Reports | Status report**. The first line of the **Status Report** shows your Drupal version number, as seen in the following exhibit:

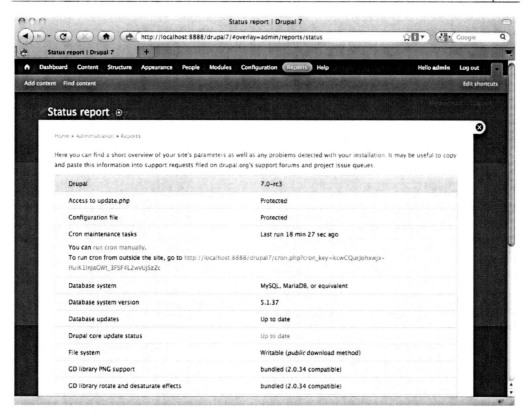

Once you know what version of Drupal you are running, you can confirm whether the theme you are considering is usable on your system. Themes normally state clearly their version compatibility. All on the themes on Drupal.org, for example, state expressly what versions of Drupal they were intended for.

 Some theme projects have multiple versions, each targeting a different Drupal release; be certain you grab the right one.

If the theme you are looking at doesn't provide versioning information, assume the worst. While it is extremely rare for a theme installation to cause problems, it's always better practice to back up your site before installing anything that might be questionable.

To back up your Drupal site properly, you need to capture three things: the core files, the /sites directory, and the database. Simply copying the files via FTP is not enough; to properly back up your site you will need to backup the database, too. To back up your database, use phpMyAdmin, or whatever tools are provided by your webhost. Alternatively there are extensions (Drupal modules) you can install on your Drupal site which allow you to perform backups from within Drupal. To learn more about the various backup techniques, visit http://drupal.org/node/22281.

Once you're past the compatibility hurdle, your next concern is whether the theme requires other components to work properly. Most themes are ready to use with your default Drupal installation, there are some themes, however, that require the installation of specific additional modules.

If the theme you've chosen requires you to download and install other extensions, the information will typically be stated on the theme's homepage or in the README file included with the theme. If additional extensions are needed, install and enable them first, before you install your theme.

By way of example, we are going to download and install one of the most popular third-party themes from Drupal.org: Zen. The authors of Zen describe the theme as "the ultimate starting theme for Drupal." Zen is very basic in design, but includes a number of useful features that make it particularly suitable for customization and extension. With Zen, you are given a selection of common templates and supporting files upon which you can build your own theme; this is typically done through the creation of a sub-theme that uses the Zen resources.

The Zen theme has been around for quite some time and is under active development. There are a lot of good resources associated with this theme and the theme is the subject of frequent discussions on the Drupal forums. The following screenshot shows the Zen project page on Drupal.org at http://drupal.org/project/zen:

Zen is not, however, the only "starter theme" out there. Drupal 7 now includes Stark, which can also be used as a starter theme (though this is not your best choice!). Other popular options include:

- **Adaptivetheme**: This package includes a wide array of options, including a ready-to-go sub-theme and its own admin theme. This is a pure CSS theme with good semantic markup and a number of configuration options for the layout and output. The Skinr module is also supported. You can find out more by visiting `http://drupal.org/project/adaptivetheme`.

- **Basic**: Originally based on Zen, the Basic theme has evolved into an independent project with its own take on the starter theme concept. It is SEO friendly and easy to modify. It also includes support for the Skinr module and for a CSS preprocessing language called SASS. To use Skinr or SASS you will need to install additional modules. You can find out more by visiting `http://drupal.org/project/basic`.

- **Framework**: A very clean and simple design intended as a "blank slate" for themers. The Framework theme is grid-based and provides good flexibility for multiple layout styles. The theme also includes a well-organized CSS and works well with mobile devices. At the time of writing, however, a Drupal 7 version was not available. You can find out more by visiting http://drupal.org/project/framework.

- **Fusion**: Fusion is a very powerful starter theme, but does require the use of the Skinr module for block styling; if you wish to use this feature, you will have to install Skinr on your site. The theme includes a wide range of options and can be used as either a flexible width or a fixed width theme. Fusion also supports the popular Superfish drop-down menus. Good documentation exists for this theme. You can find out more by visiting http://drupal.org/project/fusion.

- **Sky**: A simple CSS-based theme with support for multiple layouts. At the time of writing, a Drupal 7 version was not yet available, however one has been announced and it will supposedly include support for the Skinr module. You can find out more by visiting http://drupal.org/project/sky.

Installing an additional theme

With the arrival of Drupal 7, themes and other extensions can now be installed automatically from within the admin interface. The option to use manual installation still exists, however. We cover both options now.

Automatic installation

If your Drupal installation has access to the Internet, you can install theme files directly from Drupal.org. Alternatively, if you have downloaded the theme archive to your local machine, you can also install the theme from within the Drupal admin system, without having to manually move the files via FTP. Both options tend to be faster and simpler than traditional, manual installation.

To use the automatic installer, follow these steps:

1. First log in to the admin system and access the Theme Manager by selecting **Appearance** from the Management menu.

2. Next, when the Theme Manager loads in the overlay, select the option **Install new theme**. The automatic installer will load in the overlay, as shown in the screenshot below.

3. If you wish to install the theme directly from Drupal.org, or another location on the web, enter the URL in the field labeled **Install from a URL**. If you have already downloaded the theme archive, then click the **Browse** button, find the archive on your local computer, and then click **Open**.

4. Finally, click the **Install** button and the system will attempt to install the theme package. If you are successful you will see a confirmation message.

The theme should now be available in the Theme Manager, though at this point it will still need to be enabled before you can use it.

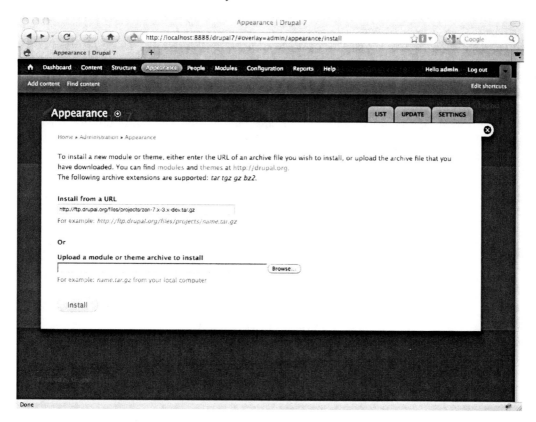

Manual installation

Manual theme installation requires that you have the ability to move files from your local machine onto your server. Typically, this is done with an FTP client or through your web hosting control panel. The method you use is up to you. It makes no difference to Drupal which method you employ.

When you obtained your theme, the odds are that it was delivered to you as a single file containing a compressed archive of files. When you download Zen you will wind up with an archive file.

The `.tar.gz` format (a.k.a. "tarball") is one of the several commonly used archive formats.

The first step towards getting the theme installed is to uncompress the archive. Double-click the archive and one of two things will happen: Either the file will uncompress and leave you with a new folder named `zen` or your system will prompt you to look for an application to open the archive file. In the latter case, you will need to track down and install a file compression program. There are lots of good ones out there. Most users, however, should have no problems as compression software is installed on many systems these days.

Once you have successfully extracted the files, take a look at what you have. If the theme directory includes a `README` file, read it now, making sure you haven't missed any system requirements or terms of use for the theme.

The next step is to get the extracted theme files on to your server. Use whatever means you prefer (FTP, control panel, and so on) to gain access to the directories of your Drupal site on the server.

Once you have access to your server, navigate to the directory `sites/all`; this is where you should place all third-party themes and modules. Place all additional theme files inside the `sites/all/themes` directory. Each theme should be kept in a separate directory. Copy the `zen` directory and its contents inside `sites/all/themes`. In this case you should have wound up with a directory structure like this: `sites/all/themes/zen`, as seen in the following exhibit:

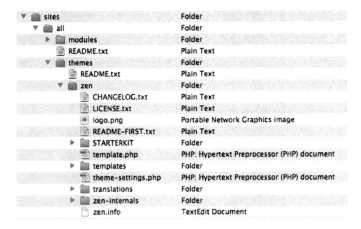

 Placing all your extensions inside the `sites/all` directory means less complication with future upgrades. Additionally, using the `sites/all/themes` directory, instead of the `themes` directory, allows you to run multiple sites off a single Drupal installation.

For the next steps, access the admin interface to your site via your browser and go to the theme. You should see your new theme listed on the page, as per the following illustration:

The Theme Manager provides a list of all the themes available on your site. Note the **Enable** link and the **Enable and set default** link; these controls are key to activating a theme for display on the site. To use the new theme we must first enable it. Once the theme is enabled, we can assign it to appear where we wish and configure it.

To enable Zen, click the **Enable** link below the theme description. Note that the appearance of the site does not change—that is because the new theme is neither assigned to any pages (nodes) nor is it set as the default.

Next, let's assign the theme to appear where we want. In this case, we want Zen to appear throughout the site, so we are going to select the **Set default** link. The **Set default** control is important; it sets the primary theme—the default theme—for the site. The default theme will be used by the system in all situations in which another theme is not specified.

Note that if we had clicked the option **Enable and set default,** the theme would have been immediately set as the default theme.

Uninstalling themes

Uninstalling themes is a simple process, essentially the reverse of installing. First go to the Themes Manager and make sure that the theme you wish to uninstall is not currently enabled. Once you have verified that it is disabled, then access your server. On the server, find the directory containing the theme files and delete the files and the directory. That's all there is to it!

Note that Drupal is very forgiving, and erroneous deletion of an active theme will not crash your site, it will simply result in the content being shown without any styling.

Summary

We started this chapter by looking at how to find and install themes and we ended by trying to extract as much as we could from a basic theme through use of the default Drupal configuration options.

As you will see in the chapters ahead, the techniques we covered in this chapter are just the beginning of what you can do with Drupal themes. Nonetheless, the configuration principles in this chapter, particularly as they relate to the use of modules and blocks and the control of visibility settings, are important for all theme work. We will come back to some of these points when we get more into heavy customization and building custom themes.

In the next chapter, we turn towards gaining a deeper understanding of how the PHPTemplate theming engine powers the Drupal presentation layer and how the features it provides can be used to best advantage.

3

Understanding PHPTemplate Themes

This chapter digs more deeply into how PHPTemplate themes function in Drupal.

The exploration of the theme files contained in this chapter lays an important foundation for understanding both how to create themes and how to modify existing themes. This chapter discusses:

- The key files used in the theming process
- How these files impact themes
- The order of precedence among theme files

Though you don't need to be fluent in PHP to understand this chapter fully, a little familiarity with the programming language will certainly make things easier. The code examples in this chapter come from the default Drupal themes, Seven and Bartik.

What is PHPTemplate?

PHPTemplate is one of a family of applications known as theme engines (sometimes referred to elsewhere as "template engines"). These applications serve a middleware function and determine the coding syntax that can be used to create a theme. As the name implies, PHPTemplate supports the popular PHP programming language for theme creation.

PHPTemplate was created specifically for use with Drupal. Though, it is not the only theming engine that can be used with Drupal, it is by far the most widely used. With the arrival of Drupal 7, PHPTemplate is so closely integrated with the Drupal core that it is extremely difficult to make a case for theming without the use of PHPTemplate.

Drupal 7 also continues a trend we saw in Drupal 6, that is, a proliferation in the number of default templates and an increase in the granularity available with those templates. In the past, there was only a limited number of default templates, and they were located directly inside the `engines` directory. Template files are now more numerous and are distributed throughout the system in a fashion that more logically reflects the templates' association with the specific modules (see *Appendix A* for a complete list).

As discussed in more detail later in this chapter, individual themes may also include theme-specific templates that appear in the theme directory of each individual theme.

 PHPTemplate files follow a naming convention ending with the file extension `.tpl.php`. For example: `block.tpl.php`, `comment.tpl.php`, `node.tpl.php`, `page.tpl.php`.

How does it all work?

Theme engines are useful tools. In addition to the role as the bridge between the functionality in the modules and the output in the presentation layer, a theme engine also helps separate the work of the programmer from the work of the designer. As a tool, PHPTemplate makes it possible for web programmers to work on the business logic of an installation without having to worry too much about the presentation of the content. In contrast, the web designers can focus entirely on the styling of discreet bits of content and items comprising the layout and the interface. Developers and designers can divide their tasks and optimize their work.

By comparison, other approaches to Drupal theming exhibit less flexibility. While themes can be created directly in PHP without the use of a theme engine, pure PHP themes are hard to decipher, more difficult to code, and awkward to preview.

Building themes that rely on the default theme engine represents the more manageable approach to handling dynamic web applications. Every PHPTemplate theme contains an HTML skeleton together with simple PHP statements that include the dynamic data. The theme files are linked to the CSS files, allowing the dynamic data to be styled and formatted with ease. Moreover PHPTemplate gives multiple options for styling your website: use simple CSS, work with themable functions, or create dedicated template files. The theme engine works in conjunction with the default templates and functions and with the theme-specific template and function overrides (if any) to produce the output the end user sees on the screen. Templates can even contain other templates, allowing you to individually control the appearance of the various elements on the page. The following illustration shows a typical template structure:

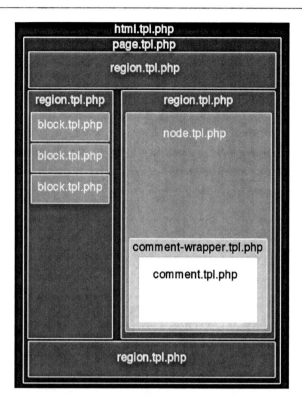

The PHPTemplate theme engine file can be found in the PHPTemplate directory on the server (themes/engines/phptemplate). Default templates and functions are located throughout the system, most frequently inside the relevant module directories. The theme-specific elements are located in the active theme's directory.

PHPTemplate theme files are written in PHP and contain a series of includes and conditional statements designed to detect the presence of elements that must be added into the final output. The includes and conditional statements relate to things such as the content of the site title, the presence and location of a logo file, the number of active regions, and so on. Whether a statement is satisfied and the content displayed is often the product of decisions made by the site administrator either in the process of configuring the site or during the creation of the site's content and functionality. The good news here is that much of the code you will see in a template file is very basic and relates purely to the formatting—CSS styling and simple HTML.

The key file in any PHPTemplate theme is `page.tpl.php`. The `page.tpl.php` file is one of the only two required files (the other being the `.info` file) to create a useful PHPTemplate theme. You can create an entire theme with only those two files, as the default templates located throughout the Drupal system will do all the work—if you let them. What normally happens, however, is that the theme also includes additional files that provide theme-specific formatting that is either unique to the theme or overrides the default styling.

The `page.tpl.php` file contains the statements that produce the output, together with the CSS styling used to control the display. The example below shows a typical application of a conditional statement to generate a specific bit of output:

```
<?php if ($site_slogan);?>
    <div id="site-slogan">
      <?php print $site_slogan; ?>
    </div>
<?php endif; ?>
```

In this segment, you see a conditional statement testing whether the `$site_slogan` returns as true (that is, it is enabled) and if so, it displays the site slogan (produced by the line `<?php print $site_slogan; ?>`).

 You will also note that the site slogan is wrapped by a `div` with an `id` of `site-slogan`. This is our first taste of how CSS integrates with the templates to control the presentation on the screen.

The preceding example code deals with Drupal's site slogan function. Whether the site slogan is displayed is determined by a parameter specified by the administrator in the Theme Configuration Manager (discussed in *Chapter 2, Working with the Default Configuration and Display Options*). The slogan text is set by the administrator in the Site Information Manager. This parameter's value is stored in the database of your Drupal site. The following exhibit shows how all these pieces work in harmony together: The choices made by the administrator are stored in the database as `$site_slogan` with the value: **This is my site slogan!**. `$site_slogan` is then displayed in courtesy of a conditional statement in the `page.tpl.php` file.

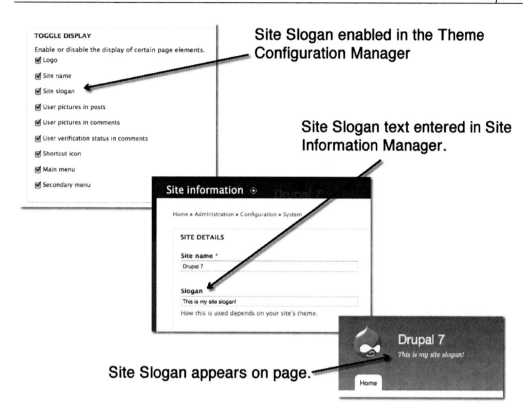

Site Slogan enabled in the Theme Configuration Manager

Site Slogan text entered in Site Information Manager.

Site Slogan appears on page.

Putting it all together, it works like this:

1. The string named `$site_slogan` is stored in the database.

2. If there is a value for `$site_slogan`, then that value will appear on the screen.

3. The user's browser applies to the resulting site slogan, the styling specified by the `div` with the `id` `"site-slogan"`.

New in Drupal 7: html.tpl.php

In previous versions of Drupal, the `page.tpl.php` file carried inside of it, the information needed to produce the basic HTML structure of the Drupal page. The `page.tpl.php` file contained the DOCTYPE, the stylesheets, the scripts, and the closing tags needed to create valid markup.

With Drupal 7 this all has changed. Those basic elements have now been removed from the `page.tpl.php` file and segregated into a new system template, `html.tpl.php`.

The new file is located in the `modules/system` directory and looks as follows:

```
?><!DOCTYPE html PUBLIC "-//W3C//DTD XHTML+RDFa 1.0//EN"
  "http://www.w3.org/MarkUp/DTD/xhtml-rdfa-1.dtd">
<html xmlns="http://www.w3.org/1999/xhtml" xml:lang="<?php print
$language->language; ?>" version="XHTML+RDFa 1.0" dir="<?php print
$language->dir; ?>"<?php print $rdf_namespaces; ?>>

<head profile="<?php print $grddl_profile; ?>">
  <?php print $head; ?>
  <title><?php print $head_title; ?></title>
  <?php print $styles; ?>
  <?php print $scripts; ?>
</head>
<body class="<?php print $classes; ?>" <?php print $attributes;?>>
  <div id="skip-link">
    <a href="#main-content" class="element-invisible element-
    focusable"><?php print t('Skip to main content'); ?></a>
  </div>
  <?php print $page_top; ?>
  <?php print $page; ?>
  <?php print $page_bottom; ?>
</body>
</html>
```

You can see in the code that in addition to the DOCTYPE and the basic HTML structure tags, the template brings in the stylesheets (`$styles`), the scripts (`$scripts`), and later in the code, the rendered page content (`$page`).

 It's not generally recommended that you override this template, but it is possible.

In the next chapter, we look at intercepting and overriding default templates.

Key PHPTemplate theme files

Let's take a deeper look at the key files involved in a PHPTemplate theme: The `.info` file and the `page.tpl.php` file. To illustrate these files at work, I will then look at how two different themes vary in their approaches.

The role of the .info file

The .info file is one of the required files in a PHPTemplate theme. This file has a configuration function and syntax similar to a .ini file. .info files are discussed in length in *Chapter 7, Dynamic Theming*, but to give you a sample of what is happening, here is the bartik.info file, which accompanies the Bartik theme (themes/bartik/bartik.info):

```
; $Id: bartik.info,v 1.5 2010/11/07 00:27:20 dries Exp $

name = Bartik
description = A flexible, recolorable theme with many regions.
package = Core
version = VERSION
core = 7.x

stylesheets[all][] = css/layout.css
stylesheets[all][] = css/style.css
stylesheets[all][] = css/colors.css
stylesheets[print][] = css/print.css

regions[header] = Header
regions[help] = Help
regions[page_top] = Page top
regions[page_bottom] = Page bottom
regions[highlighted] = Highlighted

regions[featured] = Featured
regions[content] = Content
regions[sidebar_first] = Sidebar first
regions[sidebar_second] = Sidebar second

regions[triptych_first] = Triptych first
regions[triptych_middle] = Triptych middle
regions[triptych_last] = Triptych last

regions[footer_firstcolumn] = Footer first column
regions[footer_secondcolumn] = Footer second column
regions[footer_thirdcolumn] = Footer third column
regions[footer_fourthcolumn] = Footer fourth column
regions[footer] = Footer

settings[shortcut_module_link] = 0

; Information added by drupal.org packaging script on 2011-01-05
version = "7.0"
project = "drupal"
datestamp = "1294208756"
```

Note how the file addresses basic configuration issues:

- The theme's name
- Description
- Version and compatibility info
- Theme engine required
- Stylesheets needed
- Regions included

> To learn more about the `.info` file, visit the Drupal site at `http://drupal.org/node/171205`.

The role of the page.tpl.php file

The `page.tpl.php` file, located inside the individual theme directory, plays a critical role in any PHPTemplate theme. Let's look at an example `page.tpl.php` file; in this case the default `page.tpl.php`, located in the core directory `modules/system`:

```php
<div id="page-wrapper"><div id="page">

  <div id="header"><div class="section clearfix">

    <?php if ($logo): ?>
      <a href="<?php print $front_page; ?>" title="<?php print
t('Home'); ?>" rel="home" id="logo">
        <img src="<?php print $logo; ?>" alt="<?php print t('Home');
?>" />
      </a>
    <?php endif; ?>

    <?php if ($site_name || $site_slogan): ?>
      <div id="name-and-slogan">
        <?php if ($site_name): ?>
          <?php if ($title): ?>
            <div id="site-name"><strong>
              <a href="<?php print $front_page; ?>" title="<?php
print t('Home'); ?>" rel="home"><span><?php print $site_name; ?></
span></a>
            </strong></div>
          <?php else: /* Use h1 when the content title is empty */
?>
            <h1 id="site-name">
```

```
                <a href="<?php print $front_page; ?>" title="<?php
print t('Home'); ?>" rel="home"><span><?php print $site_name; ?></
span></a>
              </h1>
          <?php endif; ?>
        <?php endif; ?>

        <?php if ($site_slogan): ?>
          <div id="site-slogan"><?php print $site_slogan; ?></div>
        <?php endif; ?>
      </div> <!-- /#name-and-slogan -->
    <?php endif; ?>

    <?php print render($page['header']); ?>

  </div></div> <!-- /.section, /#header -->

  <?php if ($main_menu || $secondary_menu): ?>
    <div id="navigation"><div class="section">
      <?php print theme('links__system_main_menu', array('links'
=> $main_menu, 'attributes' => array('id' => 'main-menu', 'class' =>
array('links', 'inline', 'clearfix')), 'heading' => t('Main menu')));
?>
      <?php print theme('links__system_secondary_menu',
array('links' => $secondary_menu, 'attributes' => array('id' =>
'secondary-menu', 'class' => array('links', 'inline', 'clearfix')),
'heading' => t('Secondary menu'))); ?>
    </div></div> <!-- /.section, /#navigation -->
  <?php endif; ?>

  <?php if ($breadcrumb): ?>
    <div id="breadcrumb"><?php print $breadcrumb; ?></div>
  <?php endif; ?>

  <?php print $messages; ?>

  <div id="main-wrapper"><div id="main" class="clearfix">

    <div id="content" class="column"><div class="section">
      <?php if ($page['highlighted']): ?><div id="highlighted"><?php
print render($page['highlighted']); ?></div><?php endif; ?>
      <a id="main-content"></a>
      <?php print render($title_prefix); ?>
      <?php if ($title): ?><h1 class="title" id="page-title"><?php
print $title; ?></h1><?php endif; ?>
      <?php print render($title_suffix); ?>
      <?php if ($tabs): ?><div class="tabs"><?php print
render($tabs); ?></div><?php endif; ?>
      <?php print render($page['help']); ?>
      <?php if ($action_links): ?><ul class="action-links"><?php
print render($action_links); ?></ul><?php endif; ?>
```

```php
      <?php print render($page['content']); ?>
      <?php print $feed_icons; ?>
    </div></div> <!-- /.section, /#content -->

    <?php if ($page['sidebar_first']): ?>
      <div id="sidebar-first" class="column sidebar"><div
class="section">
        <?php print render($page['sidebar_first']); ?>
      </div></div> <!-- /.section, /#sidebar-first -->
    <?php endif; ?>

    <?php if ($page['sidebar_second']): ?>
      <div id="sidebar-second" class="column sidebar"><div
class="section">
        <?php print render($page['sidebar_second']); ?>
      </div></div> <!-- /.section, /#sidebar-second -->
    <?php endif; ?>

  </div></div> <!-- /#main, /#main-wrapper -->

  <div id="footer"><div class="section">
    <?php print render($page['footer']); ?>
  </div></div> <!-- /.section, /#footer -->

</div></div> <!-- /#page, /#page-wrapper -->
```

Let's break down the default page.tpl.php file, and look at it in bite-sized functional units (we'll leave the CSS until the next chapter).

If you look at the code you will see that the template relies largely on conditional PHP statements to produce the output visible to the viewer. The following excerpt includes the logo, the site name, and the site slogan. As the statements are all conditional, the output will only be displayed to the site visitors, if the site administrator has enabled the items in the Theme Configuration Manager:

```php
      <?php if ($logo): ?>
        <a href="<?php print $front_page; ?>" title="<?php print
t('Home'); ?>" rel="home" id="logo">
          <img src="<?php print $logo; ?>" alt="<?php print t('Home');
?>" />
        </a>
      <?php endif; ?>

      <?php if ($site_name || $site_slogan): ?>
        <div id="name-and-slogan">
          <?php if ($site_name): ?>
            <?php if ($title): ?>
              <div id="site-name"><strong>
```

```
        <a href="<?php print $front_page; ?>" title="<?php
print t('Home'); ?>" rel="home"><span><?php print $site_name; ?></
span></a>
        </strong></div>
    <?php else: /* Use h1 when the content title is empty */
?>
    <h1 id="site-name">
        <a href="<?php print $front_page; ?>" title="<?php
print t('Home'); ?>" rel="home"><span><?php print $site_name; ?></
span></a>
    </h1>
    <?php endif; ?>
  <?php endif; ?>


  <?php if ($site_slogan): ?>
    <div id="site-slogan"><?php print $site_slogan; ?></div>
  <?php endif; ?>
 </div> <!-- /#name-and-slogan -->
<?php endif; ?>
```

Immediately following that code is the statement that prints the header region:

```
<?php print render($page['header']); ?>
```

The following lines relate to the display of the primary and secondary links:

```
<?php if ($main_menu || $secondary_menu): ?>
  <div id="navigation"><div class="section">
    <?php print theme('links__system_main_menu', array('links'
=> $main_menu, 'attributes' => array('id' => 'main-menu', 'class' =>
array('links', 'inline', 'clearfix')), 'heading' => t('Main menu')));
?>
    <?php print theme('links__system_secondary_menu',
array('links' => $secondary_menu, 'attributes' => array('id' =>
'secondary-menu', 'class' => array('links', 'inline', 'clearfix')),
'heading' => t('Secondary menu'))); ?>
  </div></div> <!-- /.section, /#navigation -->
<?php endif; ?>
```

Next, come the statements to include the breadcrumbs and the messages text:

```
<?php if ($breadcrumb): ?>
    <div id="breadcrumb"><?php print $breadcrumb; ?></div>
<?php endif; ?>


<?php print $messages; ?>
```

A little further along in the code you can see the template produce the key regions for this theme—these statements have been separated from the surrounding code to show the syntax used:

Name of region	Code including the region
Content region	`<?php print render($page['content']); ?>`
Sidebar first region	`<?php print render($page['sidebar_first']); ?>`
Sidebar second region	`<?php print render($page['sidebar_second']); ?>`
Footer region	`<?php print render($page['footer']); ?>`

In later chapters, we will look at how to enable these regions and make them eligible for block assignment.

Note how this theme uses a conditional statement to include the sidebars. The use of the conditional statement means that the sidebar columns will only display if something is assigned to the sidebar region. If nothing is assigned, then the column neatly collapses and disappears from view.

Two contrasting examples

A look at the range of techniques used by the themes in the market shows a wide variety of approaches to theming. Some themes, such as the admin-focused Seven theme, keep it simple and require only a few theme-specific elements. Other themes, such as Bartik, are more complex, and include a wide range of optional templates and stylesheets.

PHPTemplate enables you to do as little or as much as you want. If you want to create only the basics and rely on the default theming elements, you can. If you want to override the default elements with your own customized versions, you can do that, too.

The default Drupal 7 package includes two themes that demonstrate both approaches.

A simple PHPTemplate theme—Seven

The Seven theme, used for the admin system in Drupal 7, shows a direct and basic approach to the creation of a PHPTemplate theme. If you check the `themes/seven` directory on your Drupal installation, you will find the following files:

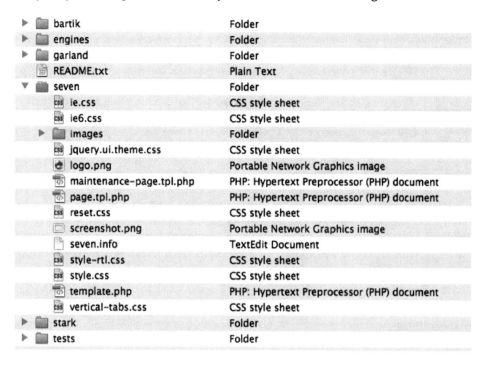

▶ 📁 bartik	Folder
▶ 📁 engines	Folder
▶ 📁 garland	Folder
📄 README.txt	Plain Text
▼ 📁 seven	Folder
📄 ie.css	CSS style sheet
📄 ie6.css	CSS style sheet
▶ 📁 images	Folder
📄 jquery.ui.theme.css	CSS style sheet
🖼 logo.png	Portable Network Graphics image
📄 maintenance-page.tpl.php	PHP: Hypertext Preprocessor (PHP) document
📄 page.tpl.php	PHP: Hypertext Preprocessor (PHP) document
📄 reset.css	CSS style sheet
🖼 screenshot.png	Portable Network Graphics image
📄 seven.info	TextEdit Document
📄 style-rtl.css	CSS style sheet
📄 style.css	CSS style sheet
📄 template.php	PHP: Hypertext Preprocessor (PHP) document
📄 vertical-tabs.css	CSS style sheet
▶ 📁 stark	Folder
▶ 📁 tests	Folder

Notice that the author of Seven has chosen to create the theme using only a basic selection of two templates: the `page.tpl.php` and `maintenance-page.tpl.php`. There is also a bare minimum of stylesheets, with several of them only coming into play in very specific circumstances, for example `ie6.css`, which helps iron out the quirks found in the rendering by the Internet Explorer 6 browser.

 Where additional templates or stylesheets are not specified, the default Drupal files are applied. The default system files provide the most basic level of formatting necessary for the styling of various page elements.

The files `page.tpl.php` and `maintenance-page.tpl.php` are alternative versions of default templates included in the core. The system will give precedence to these template files in the theme directory over the default versions of the templates, while other elements are still governed by the default templates located in the core. Put another way, the author of the Seven theme is intercepting and overriding two templates, a technique we shall explore in detail in this book—beginning in the next chapter.

> The Drupal system will give precedence to files located in the theme directory. If the theme directory contains a version of one of the default template files, the version in the theme will be used in place of the original version. By taking advantage of the feature of the Drupal system, we are able to easily intercept and override default templates and functions.

A more complex PHPTemplate theme–Bartik

By comparison, Bartik shows a more complex approach to the creation of a PHPTemplate theme. If you check the `themes/bartik` directory on the server you will find the following files. Note here that the theme developer has included not only the `page.tpl.php` file, but also his own versions of other templates, as well as a `template.php` file, and alternative `.css` files.

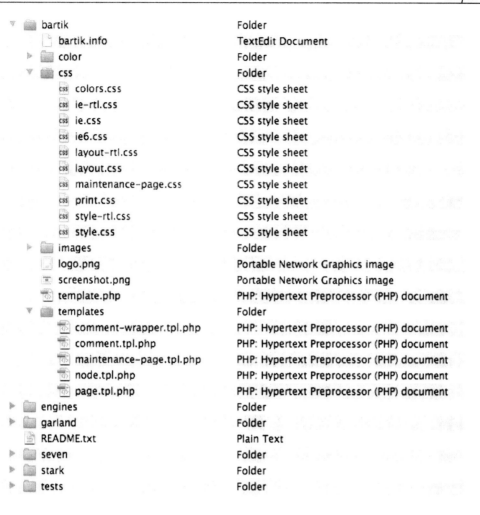

bartik	Folder
bartik.info	TextEdit Document
color	Folder
css	Folder
colors.css	CSS style sheet
ie-rtl.css	CSS style sheet
ie.css	CSS style sheet
ie6.css	CSS style sheet
layout-rtl.css	CSS style sheet
layout.css	CSS style sheet
maintenance-page.css	CSS style sheet
print.css	CSS style sheet
style-rtl.css	CSS style sheet
style.css	CSS style sheet
images	Folder
logo.png	Portable Network Graphics image
screenshot.png	Portable Network Graphics image
template.php	PHP: Hypertext Preprocessor (PHP) document
templates	Folder
comment-wrapper.tpl.php	PHP: Hypertext Preprocessor (PHP) document
comment.tpl.php	PHP: Hypertext Preprocessor (PHP) document
maintenance-page.tpl.php	PHP: Hypertext Preprocessor (PHP) document
node.tpl.php	PHP: Hypertext Preprocessor (PHP) document
page.tpl.php	PHP: Hypertext Preprocessor (PHP) document
engines	Folder
garland	Folder
README.txt	Plain Text
seven	Folder
stark	Folder
tests	Folder

The Bartik theme developer has provided the basic `page.tpl.php` file, in addition to the following optional templates:

- `comment.tpl.php`
- `comment-wrapper.tpl.php`
- `maintenance-page.tpl.php`
- `node.tpl.php`

The Bartik theme modifies only a few of the many default templates distributed with Drupal. A list of all the system's templates and themeable functions is included in the *Appendix A*.

The author of this theme also provides us with an example of another powerful Drupal theming technique: The author includes with this theme the file `template.php`. As you will see in later chapters, the `template.php` file is used to hold preprocess functions and overrides to themable functions.

Alternative theme engines

At the time of writing, the release of Drupal 7 was only briefly past. Developers of the various theme engines were still working to port their applications to Drupal. While previous Drupal releases offered a number of theme engine options, not all the alternative engines were yet compatible with Drupal 7. Engines that functioned with the Drupal 6 series are not compatible with the Drupal 7 series. Here is a quick overview of the alternatives that have existed.

PHPTAL

PHPTAL is a PHP implementation of the ZPT system. ZPT stands for Zope Page Templates. ZPT is an HTML/XML generation tool created for use in the Zope project (`http://www.zope.org`). ZPT employs **TAL (Tag Attribute Language)** to create dynamic templates. Visit the Zope site to learn more about the origins of the system, and how it all works.

TAL is attractive for several reasons. TAL statements come from XML attributes in the TAL namespace that allow you to apply TAL to an XML or plain old HTML document and enable it to function as a template. TAL generates pure, valid XHTML and the resulting template files tend to be clean and easier to read than those created with many other theme engines. One of the biggest advantages, however, is that TAL templates can be manipulated using a standard WYSIWYG HTML/XML editor and previewed in your browser, making the design work on your theme a relatively easier task.

There are several minor drawbacks to PHPTAL:

- For purists, it is one level of abstraction further away from PHP, and therefore, performs a bit slower than PHPTemplate (though this difference is unlikely to be noticed by anyone and can be overcome by proper caching).
- Installation of PHPTAL requires Pear5 and PHP5 on your server. If you lack either of these, you should explore other alternatives.

Download PHPTAL for Drupal 6.x at `http://drupal.org/project/phptal`. The Drupal extension includes a variety of extras including at least one PHPTAL theme.

Smarty

The Smarty theme engine allows you to create themes using the Smarty syntax. This popular theme engine is widely used and there are a number of pre-existing themes that are based on Smarty.

Smarty is a mature system and there exist a number of resources to help you learn Smarty's syntax and conventions. Though the system implements another scripting language inside the Drupal system (the Smarty tags), it performs very well. Smarty parses the template files at runtime and does not re-compile unless the template files change. Smarty also includes a built-in caching system to help you fine-tune performance even further. There is also a variety of plug-ins available, which allows you to extend Smarty's feature set. Download Smarty for Drupal 6.x at `http://drupal.org/project/smarty`.

Summary

In this chapter, we've looked in more depth at how PHPTemplate themes work. You should now have an awareness of the key files involved in a PHPTemplate theme and some appreciation of how those files interact. The discussion of the order of precedence among various theme files lays down a fundamental principle. You have also seen examples of two different approaches to PHPTemplate themes and how theme developers can override default theme files by placing alternative template and CSS files inside the theme directory.

In the next chapter, we dive into the world of intercepts and overrides, and see how to unlock the power of PHPTemplate themes.

4
Using Intercepts and Overrides

In this chapter, we dive into the most powerful technique for customizing the output of a Drupal site — the use of intercepts and overrides. The logical consistency of the Drupal architecture lays the foundation for the approaches discussed in this chapter. Through the application of simple naming conventions, you can intercept and override the system's default styling. By creating your own templates and selectors and then naming them properly, gaining near complete control over the output of a Drupal site is a relatively easy thing to do. The techniques discussed in this chapter enable you to customize the site as a whole or through any of its components; you can even vary the styling by type of content, page, or user.

Intercepting and overriding output can be applied to three different, but closely related, system features: templates, stylesheets (CSS), and themable functions. Though how you implement the technique varies from feature to feature, the underlying principles are exactly the same.

In this chapter, we will look at:

- The relationship between templates, stylesheets, and themable functions
- How to override styles and stylesheets
- How to override templates and themable functions
- How to use template variables

For the purpose of illustrating the examples in this chapter, we will be using the Bartik theme, bundled with your default Drupal distro.

Let's begin with the big picture — how templates, stylesheets, and themable functions work together to create the styling.

Putting together the pieces

The themes included with your Drupal system are only one part of the architecture that handles the output seen on the screen. Themes are the most accessible part of the architecture, but the real power lies in understanding the components that make up the theme and how those relate to default components that are contained elsewhere in the Drupal core.

The default Drupal system contains a large number of theming elements — templates, stylesheets, and themable functions — located outside of the theme directories. Understanding how you can work with those elements is the key to getting the most out of the system.

You've seen already that themes include a mix of files, including templates and stylesheets. You have also seen that the Drupal system includes functions that provide output and can, accordingly, be styled. To have the fullest control over your site's look and feel, you need to be fluent not only with the themes, but also with the underlying templates, stylesheets, and themable functions. Taken together, these elements provide everything the vast majority of people will need to customize a site to their needs.

As you work with Drupal over time, it is likely that you will use all of these elements at one point or another. If you are working with an existing theme, you may only modify the stylesheets to change the styling, or you may need to override a default template with a customized version of your own. Alternatively, you may want to go further and dig into the themable functions to address specific needs or create customized forms. You can do all these things (and more!) by using the elements discussed in this chapter.

Default templates

The default templates included with your Drupal system provide you with a quick and easy starting place for common customizations. Among the most powerful templates are the block and page templates, but there are many other templates located within the directories of the various modules they impact.

If you wish to customize the output of one of the templates, simply copy the template into your active theme directory and modify it as needed. Modifications can be simple, such as changing selectors, or more complex, such as adding new variables to the template.

Appendix, Identifying Templates, Stylesheets, and Themable Functions contains a listing of all the templates in the default system.

Default stylesheets

The default Drupal installation includes a mind-boggling assortment of stylesheets. If you have installed additional extensions, you may well find that they come with their own stylesheets, increasing the confusion factor even more.

While the Drupal approach to stylesheets may initially appear to be overkill in the extreme, or at the very least a rather literal application of modularization, there is a method behind the apparent madness. The use of multiple stylesheets not only makes it easier to maintain individual modules, but also helps you find what you need more quickly than having to deal with one or two massive files. The net result of the approach is actually quite effective — that is, once you come to grips with the mass of stylesheets that reside in your system!

In order to reduce the potential threats of conflicting stylesheets and absurd loading times, Drupal provides a CSS preprocessing engine. This engine identifies the required stylesheets, strips out the line breaks and spaces from all the files, and delivers the styles in a combined single file. This feature is disabled by default; if you wish to use it, you must access the Performance settings page inside the Configuration Manager and enable the option labeled **Aggregate and compress CSS files**.

 While working on the themes of your Drupal site, you should make sure the CSS compression is disabled. If the compression is enabled, you may not be able to immediately see the impact of changes to your site's CSS.

 Use of the CSS aggregation function results in the creation of a temporary CSS files inside the `sites/default/files` directory. Do not try to edit this file. While you can make changes to it, your changes will be lost as the file is temporary. Make any changes to the CSS files located in the active theme directory.

The themable functions

Themable functions are theming elements that are less complex than templates and are implemented by way of functions. There are a number of these and they are scattered throughout the system. Many are located inside of the key files of the individual modules. Drupal 7 relies less on themable functions than previous versions, but they still play a key role in theming.

> *Appendix, Identifying Templates, Stylesheets, and Themable Functions* contains a listing of all the themable functions in the default system.

The default Drupal system does not provide an automated tool for the identification of the themeable functions in Drupal. You can, however, identify them by their names; all themable functions employ a consistent naming convention. Themable functions use the prefix `theme_`. The naming convention makes it possible to work your way through the various files to isolate all the functions. You can search for them easily by setting up a tool to do the searching for you. One of the best tools is the Theme Developer module, which you can download and install on your site. To learn more go to the project page at `http://drupal.org/project/devel_themer`.

Overriding the default CSS

Drupal contains a large number of stylesheets—more than forty at the last count! While there are a lot of stylesheets to juggle, with good planning and the use of overrides, you can avoid having to track down individual stylesheets. Indeed, since you will be placing your new styles in the theme directory, you won't need to work directly with the multitude of the system's default stylesheets.

> The key is being able to identify the styles that are relevant to the elements on the screen; the Theme Developer module, or the Firebug extension for Firefox can help with that. Learn more about both of these useful theming tools in *Chapter 10, Useful Extensions for Themers.*

Drupal deals gracefully with the complexity of its multi-layered approach to CSS. The order in which the stylesheets are compiled creates a hierarchy among the stylesheets. While it is not necessary for you to be fluent with the details of the manner in which the stylesheets are compiled, it is important to appreciate the importance of the order of precedence the system employs. It is this hierarchy that enables you to easily intercept and override the default styles.

The key to intercepting and overriding styling is to take advantage of the order of precedence by defining your custom styles in last style sheet compiled. The last file compiled is highest in the hierarchy and any styles in that style sheet will override any conflicting style definitions.

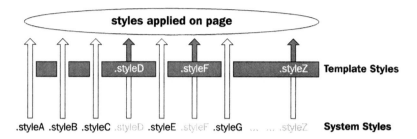

As the name implies, Cascading Stylesheets set precedence by cascade. While the last item in the cascade has the last word in the final output, don't forget that properties are also inherited. If the higher priority stylesheets do not include competing properties within the definition of a selector, then the properties from lower priority stylesheets will still be applied.

The theme's stylesheets, that is, the CSS inside the active theme directory take precedence over all other stylesheets. If there are conflicting styles definitions, the definition included in the theme's style sheet will have control. Where there is no conflict, the definitions in the default Drupal stylesheets will be applied.

 Remember, you always want to avoid modifying the default files, and that includes both the CSS files in the core and those in any additional installed modules.

Though it is not the subject of this chapter, you can also add your own stylesheets to your theme; you are not restricted to a particular file or set of files. If you wish to add additional stylesheets, you may do so by creating new stylesheets, placing them inside the theme's directory, and then incorporating them by reference inside your .info file. This topic is discussed further in *Chapter 6, Creating a New Theme* and *Chapter 8, Dealing with Forms*.

CSS overrides in action

Let's look at a basic example that illustrates the concept of overriding a default system style.

The page title in your Drupal site is styled with the selector .title. The default Bartik theme, however, contains no definition for the class .title. As there is no definition in the theme's style sheet, the system will apply the default styling to the page title.

The page title of a default Bartik installation appears as you see it in the following screenshot:

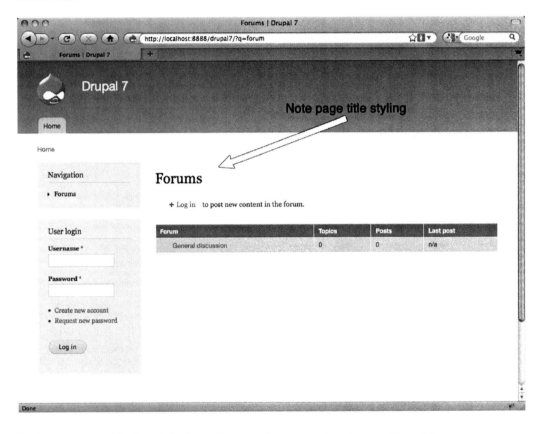

Let's now override the default styling; to do so we simply need to add our own definition for the .title class into the Bartik theme's style.css file.

For simplicity's sake, we execute this example by changing the stylesheet of one of the default themes. Note that normally you would never do this; you would instead create a sub-theme and make your changes to the sub-theme. Sub-theme creation is explained in the next chapter.

Add the following code to the Bartik theme's style sheet (`/themes/bartik/style.css`):

```
.title {
  color: #666;
  font-style: italic;
}
```

Now save the file to your server, overwriting the original `style.css` file. Our `.title` definition will now override the default styling. The results of the new styling will be seen when you reload the page in your browser, as shown in the following screenshot:

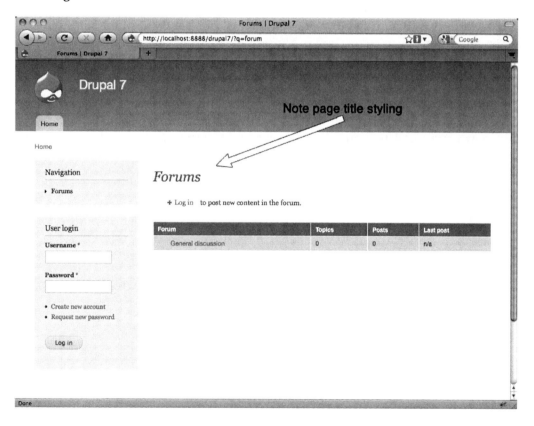

This simple example illustrates how the order of precedence allows us to easily override default style definitions—and it really is that simple. All we need to do is put our changes in the active theme directory and our styles will take precedence over the default style definitions. There's no need to make changes to the core files and no need to hunt through dozens of stylesheets to find what you need; what you need to do is find the active styles and then override them in your theme's CSS.

To override an existing style:

1. Find the styling applied to the item you want to change.
2. Write a new style definition.
3. Place the definition in the `style.css` file.
4. Repeat as needed!

Overriding core stylesheets

Just as you can override a selector by providing one of your own with the same name, you can similarly override entire stylesheets. If you wish to replace an entire core stylesheet with one of your own, you can just put a new file of the same name in the active theme. However, best practices indicate that you should not stop there. To avoid possible cascade problems and the loading of unnecessary files, you should note the change in your theme's `template.php` file.

The function `hook_css_alter()` lets you replace, add, or subtract CSS files from the page prior to the files being output. This involved a bit more work but is far cleaner and more efficient. Here is an example, taken from the Seven theme's `template. php` file. This shows `hook_css_alter()` being used to tell the system that the Seven theme is overriding two of the core stylesheets in their entirety:

```php
/**
 * Implements hook_css_alter().
 */
function seven_css_alter(&$css) {
  // Use Seven's vertical tabs style instead of the default one.
  if (isset($css['misc/vertical-tabs.css'])) {
    $css['misc/vertical-tabs.css']['data'] = drupal_get_path('theme',
'seven') . '/vertical-tabs.css';
  }
  // Use Seven's jQuery UI theme style instead of the default one.
  if (isset($css['misc/ui/jquery.ui.theme.css'])) {
    $css['misc/ui/jquery.ui.theme.css']['data'] = drupal_get_
path('theme', 'seven') . '/jquery.ui.theme.css';
  }
}
```

To learn more about the function `hook_css_alter()` visit the API page at `http://api.drupal.org/api/drupal/modules--system--system.api.php/function/hook_css_alter/7`.

Overriding templates and themable functions

The templates and themable functions employed by your site control the HTML formatting for the final display of the contents. While CSS gives you one level of control over look and feel to make significant changes to the functionality or the page layout, you will need to work with the templates or the functions.

The default templates and themable functions are located in a variety of places inside the distro. Moreover, since a theme developer can also create theme-specific templates and themable functions, you may find these items located inside the active theme's directory.

Like CSS styles, all templates and themable functions in a Drupal site can be overridden. As we saw with stylesheets, there is a hierarchy at work inside Drupal. The system will seek out functions and templates in a specific order, and apply the first one it finds.

Note that we're seeing a trend in Drupal naming conventions, with more and more people (and some parts of the Drupal documentation) now referring to templates and functions by the generic term "hooks." While the label is accurate, it isn't very specific and for the purposes of this book, we will continue to specify whether we are talking about a template or a function.

Various approaches to overriding the Default Styling

There are various ways you can override the templates and functions. Each of the approaches has advantages and disadvantages and you, as the theme developer, will need to decide which approach best suits your needs.

The various approaches are:

* Overriding templates

- Overriding functions
- Converting themable functions into new templates

In the following sections, we will look at each of these approaches.

The Theme Registry

The Theme Registry provides the Drupal system with a cached registry of information on the available functions and templates. When you add or remove theme functions or templates, you need to force the system to update the Theme Registry. (Simply editing an existing function or template, however, does not require you to clear the Registry.)

To update the Registry:

1. Go to the **Configuration Manager**.

2. Visit the **Performance** page.

3. Select the option **Clear cached data**.

(If you have the Devel module installed, you can access this link more quickly by enabling the Devel Block.)

This is an important step that should not be skipped, else you may not be able to see your changes.

Overriding templates

This is an easy and powerful technique for managing customization. The essence of this approach is to create a duplicate of one of the default template files and then place it in the active theme's directory. The new files will intercept the default template and override it as Drupal will always display the template in the active directory rather than the default template.

The process of applying this technique is a straightforward matter of creating a duplicate for the file, and then modifying the code inside the new file:

1. Identify the template you need.

2. Copy the template you wish to customize.

3. Paste the template into the theme directory, being careful to maintain the original file name.

4. Make your changes to the code in the new template file.

5. Save the file.

6. Clear the Theme Registry.

By applying the technique in this manner, you are able to make your changes without having to modify the original core files. In the future, you benefit from this when it comes to upgrading your Drupal site, because you do not have to worry about the core upgrade overwriting your modifications. Additionally, your modified files are portable: Should you wish to apply these changes to another theme, you only need to copy the appropriate files into the theme's directory.

Up to this point, we have limited the discussion to overriding of the default (global) template files and individual functions. However in Drupal, you can extend the intercept and override concept further to achieve highly granular control of the page templates that are called in various situations. You can, in other words, intercept and override on a conditional basis.

For example, if you wish to have different templates used for different types of content, you can create template files that are displayed only when that content is displayed. You can also style individual incidents of modules and other output using the techniques described in this chapter.

Let's look at one of the most common uses of this technique: The `page.tpl.php` file is one of the most important in a PHPTemplate theme. This file is largely responsible for the results that appear in the browser—it defines the overall layout of a page of your site. As you might expect given the name of the file, it appears in a wide variety of situations—it is the default page template.

Given the ubiquity of the file, there could be times when you want to customize a particular page (or set of pages) to add variety to your site or to enhance usability. To accomplish this task, you don't need to install another theme, instead, you simply create another version of the existing `page.tpl.php` file and tailor it to display when certain conditions are met. To control the display of the new template, we will turn once again to Drupal's hierarchies and naming conventions.

The above approach is also commonly referred to as using "template suggestions."

Let's assume you wish to customize the user pages, that is, the page seen when a user selects the **My account** link. In the absence of any special definitions, Drupal will use the `page.tpl.php` file. If you want a custom page to be displayed, you will need to intercept the default page and display the page of your choosing. To do so, you will need to create a new template named `page--user.tpl.php` and place it in the active theme's directory. Now, when a user clicks on the **My account** link, the system will display the file `page--user.tpl.php` rather than the default `page.tpl.php` file. Note that the syntax for naming template suggestions has changed in Drupal 7. In the past, only one dash character was used. With Drupal 7, you now have to use the "double-dash" to specify a suggestion. The single dash is only used to separate two-part names.

Taking this one step further, let's say you want to show a particular user a customized user page. In that case, you would create a new template based on the `page.tpl.php` file and name it so that it carries the user's ID, for example, `page--user-1.tpl.php` (in this case, displaying the template to the user whose ID=1 when they view the user page).

The logical, hierarchical nature of the system gives theme developers a great deal of control over pages or elements of pages. Drupal is consistent and the same logic applies throughout the system: The system prefers the specific to the general. Drupal looks first for the most specific definition, and where that is absent, cascades downward, finally displaying the default instance where nothing else is found.

The illustration shows how template suggestions can intercept and override the default templates. The hierarchy works from specific to general, where the specific takes precedence over the general.

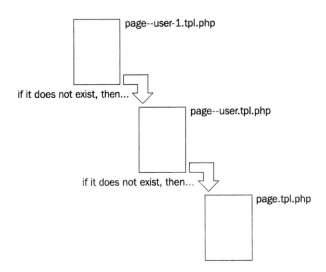

By extension, the same principle can be applied to any `tpl.php` file. For example, a common request is for node-specific styling, for example, having a unique template tailored to the Blog content type. To achieve variable styling according to node, you employ the same approach: Create the needed `tpl.php` files (applying the naming convention) and place them in the theme directory. At runtime, Drupal will call the appropriate files.

For more information on this subject, as well as examples, please refer to *Chapter 7, Dynamic Theming*.

Overriding functions

Themable functions are located in a variety of places throughout the system, most typically inside the various modules. Themable functions can be overridden by copying the functions and placing them in the active theme's template.php file, where they can be modified to suit your needs.

The template.php file is an optional file in a PHPTemplate theme. When this file is present, Drupal will look in this file for extra instructions. This file provides a convenient place to define overrides of functions (among other things, like preprocessing functions).

Here's a quick overview on the process used to implement this technique:

1. If it does not exist, create a new file named template.php inside your theme directory (use proper PHP syntax).

2. Find the function you wish to customize.

3. Copy the original function and paste it into the template.php file.

4. Rename the function (as discussed below).

5. Make your changes to the renamed function in the template.php file and save the file.

6. Clear the Theme Registry.

Again, note that by putting the changes inside a file in your theme directory, you can add customization to a site without having to touch the core files. Another significant advantage of this approach is simplicity: You can have one file (template.php) that can be used to hold multiple overrides. This approach makes it easy to locate your themable function overrides and manage them. The downside is that this is a theme-specific approach to the issue of overrides; should your site employ more than one theme, this approach may not be optimal.

 Note that using functions has one clear advantage: In terms of site performance, functions tend to be marginally faster than templates.

The themable function hierarchy is invoked through the use of a naming convention. The default themable functions can be identified by their names; all employ the nomenclature `theme_functionname()`. For example, the default themable function that controls the output of a Drupal breadcrumb trail is named `theme_breadcrumb()`.

 The default breadcrumb function is located in the `includes/theme.inc` file. We will be looking at this function in more detail later in this chapter.

At runtime, Drupal is designed to look for overrides to themable functions before applying the default functions. The system does this by looking for functions in the following order (assuming your site employs the PHPTemplate engine):

- `themename_functionname` (for example, `bartik_breadcrumb`)
- `theme_functionname` (for example, `theme_breadcrumb`)

 The naming convention is the key to your files being found and used properly, so it must be followed scrupulously.

If the system does not find a function employing the specific theme namespace, the system will apply the default function.

Converting themable functions into dedicated templates

The final technique to master is the creation of individual template files that are dedicated to overriding specific themable functions. Transforming a function into a new template file gives you more flexibility than simply modifying the function inside the `template.php` file. By creating templates out of themable functions, you can strip down the function to its themable elements and make the theming more accessible. Separate templates tend to be easier to work with, particularly for those less fluent in PHP.

 If you are a developer working with a designer, you can use this approach to break the themable elements into bite-sized pieces, and then pass them over to the designer for work on the look and feel. You can focus on the functionality; the designer can focus on the presentation layer.

The steps are as follows:

1. Create a new .tpl.php file inside your theme directory.

2. Name the new file by taking the function name, dropping the prefix, and changing the underscores to dashes (also known as "hyphens"). For example, the function theme_comment_view would become the template comment-view.tpl.php.

3. Paste into the new file the code from the function that relates to the formatting and the output.

4. Make your changes to the file's code.

5. Save the file.

6. Clear the Theme Registry.

Let's look at an example.

Suppose you would like to have a dedicated file for the breadcrumb function. The name of the breadcrumb function is theme_breadcrumb. The original function is located at includes/theme.inc.

Let's start by looking at the original function:

```
/**
 * Returns HTML for a breadcrumb trail.
 *
 * @param $variables
 *    An associative array containing:
 *    - breadcrumb: An array containing the breadcrumb links.
 */
function theme_breadcrumb($variables) {
  $breadcrumb = $variables['breadcrumb'];

  if (!empty($breadcrumb)) {
    // Provide a navigational heading to give context for breadcrumb
links to
    // screen-reader users. Make the heading invisible with .element-
invisible.
    $output = '<h2 class="element-invisible">' . t('You are here') .
'</h2>';

    $output .= '<div class="breadcrumb">' . implode(' » ',
$breadcrumb) . '</div>';
    return $output;
  }
}
```

We'll need to extract the portion of that function that relates to the output and place that into the template, adding the styling of our choice. In this example, I want to go ahead make the `You are here` text visible to everyone, I want all the output on one line, and I want to wrap it in divs for easy styling.

Here's how it can be done:

1. Create a new file, place it inside the Bartik theme directory and name it `breadcrumb.tpl.php`.

2. Enter the following lines of code into your new `breadcrumb.tpl.php` file:

   ```
   <div><span class="breadcrumb-title"><?php print t('You are here
   :'); ?></span>
   <span class="breadcrumb"><?php print implode(' » ', $breadcrumb);
   ?></span></div>
   ```

3. Save the file.

After you clear the site's Registry and refresh your browser, you will be able to see your new breadcrumb layout.

Note that the code is basic HTML styling wrapped around PHP `print` statements. This sort of basic code should be relatively easier for many people to deal with, as opposed to trying to extract the relevant statement from the more complicated function code (as you would have to do if you simply dropped all your function overrides into the `template.php` file). All the designer needs to do now is provide the desired definitions for the two CSS selectors, 'breadcrumb-title' and 'breadcrumb'.

Overrides in Action: A look at overrides in Bartik

Let's have a look at how Drupal's default Bartik theme handles overrides. The author of Bartik employs a number of overrides and the ways in which they are implemented provide us with some easily accessible examples of overrides in action.

A look inside the `themes/` directory shows the structure employed by Bartik and gives us hints to this theme's approach to overrides. There's a directory dedicated to holding the theme's numerous CSS files, another to hold the theme-specific templates and you will also note the presence of a `template.php` file. In other words, the Bartik theme has employed a mix of the approaches that I've discussed throughout this chapter.

Overriding the default template files

Bartik includes alternative versions of several default template files. The contents of each of those files vary from their counterparts of the same name located elsewhere in the core.

Bartik employs the PHPTemplate engine, accordingly when you open the /templates directory you will note a number of files with the .tpl.php extension. In addition to the basic page.tpl.php file, Bartik includes alternative versions of the following default templates. Here's a list of the default templates the Bartik author overrides, along with the locations of the original files:

Template	Original location
comment.tpl.php	/modules/comment/
Comment-wrapper.tpl.php	/modules/comment/
node.tpl.php	/modules/node/
maintenance-page.tpl.php	/modules/system/

By way of example, let's compare the default version of the node.tpl.php file with Bartik's modified version of the node.tpl.php file.

In the default template you will find the following code:

```
<div id="node-<?php print $node->nid; ?>" class="<?php print $classes;
?> clearfix"<?php print $attributes; ?>>

<?php print $user_picture; ?>

<?php print render($title_prefix); ?>
<?php if (!$page): ?>
<h2<?php print $title_attributes; ?>><a href="<?php print $node_url;
?>"><?php print $title; ?></a></h2>
<?php endif; ?>
<?php print render($title_suffix); ?>

<?php if ($display_submitted): ?>
<div class="submitted">
<?php print $submitted; ?>
</div>
<?php endif; ?>

<div class="content"<?php print $content_attributes; ?>>
<?php
      // We hide the comments and links now so that we can render them
later.
      hide($content['comments']);
      hide($content['links']);
```

```
        print render($content);
    ?>
</div>

<?php print render($content['links']); ?>

<?php print render($content['comments']); ?>

</div>
```

The version of node.tpl.php included in the Bartik theme directory looks like this:

```
<div id="node-<?php print $node->nid; ?>" class="<?php print $classes;
?> clearfix"<?php print $attributes; ?>>

<?php print render($title_prefix); ?>
<?php if (!$page): ?>
<h2<?php print $title_attributes; ?>>
<a href="<?php print $node_url; ?>"><?php print $title; ?></a>
</h2>
<?php endif; ?>
<?php print render($title_suffix); ?>

<?php if ($display_submitted): ?>
<div class="meta submitted">
<?php print $user_picture; ?>
<?php print $submitted; ?>
</div>
<?php endif; ?>

<div class="content clearfix"<?php print $content_attributes; ?>>
<?php
    // We hide the comments and links now so that we can render them
later.
    hide($content['comments']);
    hide($content['links']);
    print render($content);
?>
</div>

<?php
    // Remove the "Add new comment" link on the teaser page or if the
comment
    // form is being displayed on the same page.
    if ($teaser || !empty($content['comments']['comment_form'])) {
      unset($content['links']['comment']['#links']['comment-add']);
    }
    // Only display the wrapper div if there are links.
    $links = render($content['links']);
    if ($links):
```

```
    ?>
<div class="link-wrapper">
<?php print $links; ?>
</div>
<?php endif; ?>

<?php print render($content['comments']); ?>

</div>
```

The two versions of the template look very similar, but there are several differences:

- The Bartik theme moves the placement of the user picture
- Bartik adds custom styling in several places
- Bartik adds logic that changes the handling of the **Add new comment** link

When the Bartik theme is active, the Drupal system will apply Bartik's version of node.tpl.php and ignore the default file of the same name in the modules/node/ directory. The modified file in the Bartik theme takes precedence over the default file of the same name.

The author uses the same technique with the other files in the /templates directory, providing in these files alternative formatting to that included in the default templates. Compare and contrast those files to view the differences.

Overriding themable functions

In addition to providing substitutes for some of the default template files, the Bartik author has also included a template.php file, which includes both themable function overrides and template preprocessing functions.

 Preprocessing functions are used to modify existing variables or to create new variables that can be used by the theming system. Preprocessing functions are discussed in more detail in later chapters.

Let's look at an example: If you open the template.php file and examine the contents, you will find an override to one of Drupal's themable functions: theme_menu_tree().

It's useful to compare and contrast the original with the override.

The original function theme_menu_item() is located in /includes/menu.inc and looks like this:

```
function theme_menu_tree($variables) {
```

```
        return '<ul class="menu">' . $variables['tree'] . '</ul>';
```

The override is named `bartik_menu_tree` and resides in `template.php`. It looks like this:

```
    function bartik_menu_tree($variables) {
        return '<ul class="menu clearfix">' . $variables['tree'] . '</ul>';
```

Note the theme author has simply changed the selector applied to the function.

While the Bartik author could have achieved the same result by converting the function into a template, I think you will agree that in this case creating an override inside `template.php` is a more sensible approach than creating a dedicated template. A simple change such as this really does not deserve the creation of a template, unless of course you are preparing things for someone who is completely PHP unfriendly.

We encourage you to explore further Bartik's `template.php` file; there are more things you can learn from seeing how the Bartik developers approached the creation of the theme, but for my purposes, the above examples are sufficient to provide the foundation we need to move on.

Working with template variables

As we have seen previously, Drupal templates often rely upon variables that are used to enhance and extend the functionality. The default Drupal variables cover the most common (and essential) functions. Some of the Drupal variables are unique to particular templates, others are common to all. In addition to the default variables, you can also define your own variables.

Drupal 7 provides two opportunities for adding, deleting, or overriding the variables for your templates. The template variables can be manipulated through the use of either the process or preprocess functions. These functions are run prior to the template being displayed, thereby allowing you to manipulate the variables for use in the templates themselves. The use of variables process functions is an efficient approach for handling logic needed for your theme and preferable to adding processing logic inside your template files.

 The `template_process()` function is a new addition in Drupal 7. In Drupal 6, your only option was the `template_preprocess()` function.

Variables created through the use of the functions can be used by any of your templates. Note that the preprocess functions only apply to theming hooks implemented as templates; plain theme functions do not interact with the preprocessors.

In Drupal 5 and lower versions, the function _phptemplate_ variables served the same purpose as the preprocess function. For a list of the expected preprocess functions and their order of precedence, see http://drupal.org/node/223430.

Typically, if you wish to implement a variables process function for your theme, you will add one (or more) of the following to your template.php file.

Name of preprocessor	Application
[themeName]_preprocess	Will apply to all hooks. This will run before the process functions, if any.
[themeName]_preprocess_[hookname]	Specific to a single hook. This will run before the process functions, if any.
[themeName]_process	Will apply to all hooks. This will run after the preprocess functions, if any.
[themeName]_process_[hookname]	Specific to a single hook. This will run after the preprocess functions, if any.

When creating a function that specifies a hook name, the majority of the time you will be naming a specific template. Note that the system only permits you to name the base template; it is not possible to name template suggestions.

Let's look first at intercepting and overriding a default variable and then at creating a new variable.

Intercepting and overriding variables

You can intercept and override the system's existing variables. Intercepting a variable is no different in practice from intercepting a themable function: You simply restate it in the template.php file and make your modifications there, leaving the original code in the core intact.

To intercept an existing variable and override it with your new variable, you need to use the function, add the function to your `template.php` file, according to the following syntax:

```php
<?php
function themename_preprocess(&$vars) {
  $vars['name'] = add your code here...;
  }
?>
```

Note that nothing should be returned from these functions. The variables have to be passed by reference, as indicated by the ampersand before variables, for example, `&$vars`.

Let's take a very basic example and apply this. Let's override `$title` in `page.tpl.php`. To accomplish this task, add the following code to the `template.php` file:

```php
<?php
function themename_preprocess(&$vars) {
  $vars['title'] = 'override title';
  }
?>
```

Remember to clear your theme registry after you save your changes!

With this change made and the file saved to your theme, the string **override title** will appear, substituted for the original `$title` value.

Making new variables available

The variables process functions also allow you to define additional variables in your theme. To create a new variable, you must declare the function in the `template.php` file. In order for your theme to have its preprocessors recognized, the template associated with the hook must exist inside the theme. If the template does not exist in your theme, copy (or create) one and place it in the theme directory.

The syntax is the same as that just used for intercepting and overriding a variable, as seen above. The ability to add new variables to the system is a powerful tool and gives you the ability to add more complex logic to your theme.

By way of example, let's assume you want to add a disclaimer statement to all the comments posted on your site. First, let's make the variable available to your templates. To do this, add the following to your `template.php` file:

```php
<?php
function bartik_gnu_preprocess(&$vars){
   $vars['disclaimer'] = t('Comments are unmoderated. The views
expressed are those of the comment author.');
}
?>
```

You now have a new variable named `disclaimer`.

Note that we've included the `t` function to provide for translation of the new string. This is exactly the sort of processing you want to place outside the templates themselves.

Next, to get the disclaimer statement to appear on your comments, open the `comment-wrapper.tpl.php` file and add the following before the closing div:

```php
<p><?php print $disclaimer; ?></p>
```

Flush your caches and then load a page upon which you have comments enabled. You should see the new disclaimer text at the bottom of the comment form.

The preceding example is a simple one. You can make your variables as simple or as complex as you see fit; the principles remain the same.

 The Drupal API contains more information on template process and preprocess functions. See `http://api.drupal.org/api/drupal/includes--theme.inc/function/theme/7` for more details.

Summary

Intercepts and overrides are your most powerful techniques for controlling Drupal site output. In this chapter, we covered how to intercept and override the default Drupal CSS, the themable functions, and the templates.

The techniques discussed require an understanding of Drupal naming conventions and an appreciation for the hierarchies that dictate precedence. Proper use of the naming conventions will enable you to extensively customize Drupal's appearance.

This chapter also includes a review of various alternative techniques for handling themable functions, together with the advantages of each. If you engage in a bit of planning, the step-by-step instructions introduced in this chapter should allow you to get started with overrides and to even create some conditional styling.

In the next chapter, we take an in-depth look at techniques for customizing an existing theme.

5
Customizing an Existing Theme

With the arrival of Drupal 6, sub-theming really came to the forefront of theme design. While previously many people copied themes and then re-worked them to achieve their goals, that process became less attractive as sub-themes came into favor. This chapter focuses on sub-theming and how it should be used to customize an existing theme.

For the purpose of illustrating the examples in this chapter, we'll be using the Bartik theme, which is included in the default Drupal 7 package. Among the topics we will cover:

- Selecting a base theme
- Creating a sub-theme
- Customizing your sub-theme

We'll start by looking at how to set up a workspace for Drupal theming.

Setting up the workspace

Before you get too far into attempting to modify your theme files, you should put some thought into your tools. There are several software applications that can make your work modifying themes more efficient. Though no specific tools are required to work with Drupal themes, you could do it all with just a text editor—there are a couple of applications that you might want to consider adding to your tool kit.

The first item to consider is browser selection. Firefox has a variety of extensions that make working with themes easier. The Web Developer extension, for example, is hugely helpful when dealing with CSS and related issues. We recommend the combination of Firefox and the Web developer extension to anyone working with Drupal themes. Another extension popular with many developers is Firebug, which is very similar to the Web developer extension, and is indeed more powerful in several regards.

Pick up Web developer, Firebug, and other popular Firefox add-ons at `https://addons.mozilla.org/en-US/firefox/`.

There are also certain utilities you can add into your Drupal installation that will assist with theming the site. Two modules you definitely will want to install are Devel and Theme developer. Theme developer can save you untold hours of digging around trying to find the right function or template. When the module is active all you need to do is click on an element and the Theme developer pop-up window will show you what is generating the element, along with other useful information like potential template suggestions. The Devel module performs a number of functions and is a prerequisite for running Theme developer.

Download Devel from: `http://drupal.org/project/devel`. You can find Theme developer at: `http://drupal.org/project/devel_themer`.

Note that neither Devel nor Theme Developer are suitable for use in a development environment—you don't want these installed and enabled on a client's public site, as they can present a security risk.

When it comes to working with PHP files and the various theme files, you will also need a good code editor. There's a whole world of options out there, and the right choice for you is really a personal decision. Suffice it to say: as long as you are comfortable with it, it's probably the right choice.

Setting up a local development server

Another key component of your workspace is the ability to preview your work—preferably locally. As a practical matter, previewing Drupal themes requires the use of a server; themes are difficult to preview with any accuracy without a server to execute the PHP code. While you can work on a remote server on your webhost, often this is undesirable due to latency or simple lack of availability. A quick solution to this problem is to set up a local server using something like the XAMPP package (or the MAMP package for Mac OSX).

XAMPP provides a one step installer containing everything you need to set up a server environment on your local machine (Apache, MySQL, PHP, phpMyAdmin, and more). Visit `http://www.ApacheFriends.org` to download XAMPP and you can have your own Dev Server set up on your local machine in no time at all.

Follow these steps to acquire the XAMPP installation package and get it set up on your local machine:

1. Connect to the Internet and direct your browser to `http://www.apachefriends.org`.

2. Select XAMPP from the main menu.

3. Click the link labeled **XAMPP for Windows**.

4. Click the `.zip` option under the heading **XAMPP for Windows**.

5. Note that you will be re-directed to the SourceForge site for the actual download.

6. When the pop-up prompts you to save the file, click OK and the installer will download to your computer.

7. Locate the downloaded archive (`.zip`) package on your local machine, and double-click it.

8. Double-click the new file to start the installer.

9. Follow the steps in the installer and then click **Finish** to close the installer.

That's all there is to it. You now have all the elements you need for your own local development server.

To begin, simply open the XAMPP application and you will see buttons that allow you to start the servers.

To create a new website, simply copy the files into a directory placed inside the /htdocs directory. You can then access your new site by opening the URL in your browser, as follows: http://localhost/sitedirectoryname.

As a final note, you may also want to have access to a graphics program to handle editing any image files that might be part of your theme. Again, there is a world of options out there and the right choice is up to you.

Planning the modifications

A proper dissertation on site planning and usability is beyond the scope of this book. Similarly, this book is neither an HTML nor a CSS tutorial; accordingly, in this chapter we are going to focus on identifying the issues and delineating the process involved in the customization of an existing theme, rather than focusing on design techniques or coding-specific changes.

Any time you set off down the path of transforming an existing theme into something new, you need to spend some time planning. The principle here is the same as in many other areas. A little time spent planning at the frontend of a project can pay off big in savings later.

When it comes to planning your theming efforts, the very first question you have to answer is whether you are going to customize an existing theme or whether you will create a new theme. In either event, it is recommended that you work with sub-themes. The key difference is the nature of the base theme you select, that is, the theme you are going to choose as your starting point.

Chapter 6, Creating a New Theme, deals with the topic of creating new themes.

In sub-theming, the base theme is the starting point. Sub-themes inherit the parent theme's resources; hence, the base theme you select will shape your theme building. Some base themes are extremely simple, designed to impose on the themer the fewest restrictions; others are designed to give you the widest range of resources to assist your efforts. However, since you can use any theme for a base theme, the reality is that most themes fall in between, at least in terms of their suitability for use as a base theme.

Another way to think of the relationship between a base theme and a sub-theme is in terms of a parent-child relationship. The child (sub-theme) inherits its characteristics from its parent (the base theme). There are no limits to the ability to chain together multiple parent-child relationships; a sub-theme can be the child of another sub-theme.

When it comes to customizing an existing theme, the reality is often that the selection of the base theme will be dictated by the theme's default appearance and feature set; in other words, you are likely to select the theme that is already the closest to what you want. That said, don't limit yourself to a shallow surface examination of the theme. In order to make the best decision, you need to look carefully at the underlying theme's file and structures and see if it truly is the best choice. While the original theme may be fairly close to what you want, it may also have limitations that require work to overcome. Sometimes it is actually faster to start with a more generic theme that you already know and can work with easily. Learning someone else's code is always a bit of a chore and themes are like any other code—some are great, some are poor, most are simply okay. A best practices theme makes your life easier.

 In *Chapter 6, Creating a New Theme*, I list a number of third-party base themes that are great starting points for themers.

In simplest terms, the process of customizing an existing theme can be broken into three steps:

1. Select your base theme.
2. Create a sub-theme from your base theme.
3. Make the changes to your new sub-theme.

Why it is not recommended to simply modify the theme directly? There are two following reasons:

- First, best practices say not to touch the original files; leave them intact so you can upgrade them without losing customizations.
- Second, as a matter of theming philosophy, it's better to leave the things you don't need to change in the base theme and focus your sub-theme on only the things you want to change. This approach to theming is more manageable and makes for much easier testing as you go.

Selecting a base theme

For the sake of simplicity, in this chapter we are going to work with the default Bartik theme. We'll take Bartik, create a new sub-theme and then modify the sub-theme to create the customized theme. Let's call the new theme "JeanB".

 Note that while we've named the theme "JeanB", when it comes to naming the theme's directory, we will use "jeanb" as the system only supports lowercase letters and underscores.

 In order to make the example easier to follow and to avoid the need to install a variety of third-party extensions, the modifications we will make in this chapter will be done using only the default components. Arguably, when you are building a site like this for deployment in the real world (rather than simply for skills development) you might wish to consider implementing one or more specialized third-party extensions to handle certain tasks. See *Chapter 10, Useful Extensions for Themers* for a discussion of useful extensions that aid solving common site building issues.

Creating a new sub-theme

The steps involved in creating a new sub-theme are detailed as follows, but in a nutshell, it works like this:

1. Make a copy of the theme directory (and its contents).
2. Rename the directory.
3. Delete the files you don't need.
4. Update the theme name inside the files you want to keep.
5. Create a new stylesheet.
6. Update the `.info` file.

So, let's get started.

Create a copy of the base theme

Access your Drupal installation on your server, and then make a copy of the Bartik theme directory (located at `/themes/bartik`).

Create the sub-theme in a new directory

Paste the copy of the directory containing the Bartik files into the `/sites/all/themes` directory and rename it to reflect our new theme's name: *jeanb*. So you should now have a new directory at: `sites/all/themes/jeanb`.

Delete the files you don't need

Our sub-theme will inherit mostly everything from the base theme. The exception being the `.info` file (and a new stylesheet that we will create later). Given that inheritance is the norm, you should eliminate everything from the sub-theme that you don't plan to change. In other words, if there's no change planned for the file, delete it from the sub-theme's directory.

For purposes of this example, let's assume that we want to add a custom template for the front page and that we need the `template.php` file for some themable function overrides. Given those requirements, let's keep those two files, plus our `.info` file, and let's get rid of everything else. The next step, therefore, is to open up our new directory and delete everything except `.info`, `/templates/page.tpl.php`, and `template.php`. Also keep the `/css` directory, but delete all the contents; we will use that directory to hold our sub-theme's new CSS files.

Note that there's no reason to keep all that stuff inside the `template.php` file; go ahead and clean out the file. If you decide at a later stage to override any of the file contents, you can always copy it from the original file and add it to our new `template.php`. Go ahead and clean out your `template.php` file now—leave only the `<?php` at the top (that's important!).

Update the theme name throughout the sub-theme

We need to change every occurrence of "bartik" in our sub-theme to "jeanb". If you've got a code editor, you can run a find/replace to get this done, if not, you'll need to crack open each file and do this.

Create a stylesheet for your sub-theme

Next, let's create a new `.css` file. This is a requirement for a valid sub-theme; you need at least one stylesheet. Create an empty file, name it `jeanb.css`, and put it in the `/css` directory.

Update the sub-theme's .info file

The final step in the process is to update your .info file. First, rename it jeanb.info (if you have not already done so when you changed all the occurrences of "bartik" to "jeanb".) Next, open up the file and perform the following operations on the contents:

1. Make sure the name has been updated.

2. Update the description line as you see fit – this information will appear inside the Theme Manager as a description for the theme.

3. Delete the lines for package, version, and core.

4. Add a new line: base theme = bartik.

5. Declare our new stylesheet by adding this line: stylesheets[all] [] = css/ jeanb.css.

6. Delete all other stylesheet declarations.

7. Save the file.

At the end of this process, your jeanb.info file should look like this:

```
; $Id: bartik.info,v 1.5 2010/11/07 00:27:20 dries Exp $

name = JeanB
description = A new sub-theme based on Bartik.
base theme = bartik
engine = phptemplate

stylesheets[all][] = css/jeanb.css

regions[header] = Header
regions[help] = Help
regions[page_top] = Page top
regions[page_bottom] = Page bottom
regions[highlighted] = Highlighted

regions[featured] = Featured
regions[content] = Content
regions[sidebar_first] = Sidebar first
regions[sidebar_second] = Sidebar second

regions[triptych_first] = Triptych first
regions[triptych_middle] = Triptych middle
regions[triptych_last] = Triptych last

regions[footer_firstcolumn] = Footer first column
regions[footer_secondcolumn] = Footer second column
regions[footer_thirdcolumn] = Footer third column
regions[footer_fourthcolumn] = Footer fourth column
regions[footer] = Footer
```

```
settings[shortcut_module_link] = 0

; Information added by drupal.org packaging script on 2011-01-05
version = "7.0"
project = "drupal"
datestamp = "1294208756"
```

 Note that sub-themes do not inherit custom regions from the parent theme. Therefore if you want to use the custom regions in the original Bartik, you will need to re-specify them, as you can see in the preceding .info file.

Additionally, your /sites/all/themes directory should look like the following:

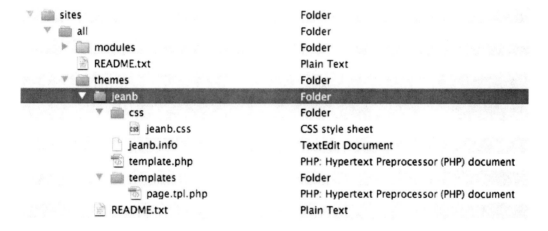

▼ sites	Folder	
▼ all	Folder	
▶ modules	Folder	
README.txt	Plain Text	
▼ themes	Folder	
▼ jeanb	Folder	
▼ css	Folder	
css jeanb.css	CSS style sheet	
jeanb.info	TextEdit Document	
template.php	PHP: Hypertext Preprocessor (PHP) document	
▼ templates	Folder	
page.tpl.php	PHP: Hypertext Preprocessor (PHP) document	
README.txt	Plain Text	

If all has gone according to plan, the new JeanB can now been seen inside the **Disabled Themes** section of your site's Theme Manager, as shown in the following figure:

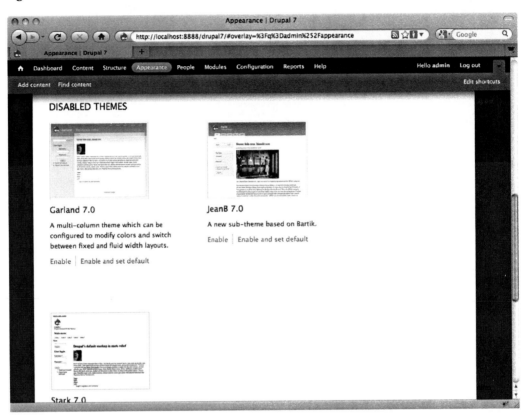

At this point, go ahead and make the theme visible on the site so that you can see the impact of my work. To do this, select the option to **Enable and set default** from the links that you see immediately below JeanB in the previous screenshot.

If you view the frontend of the site, you will see that there is a very little difference between the presentation of your new JeanB and the original Bartik. One thing you will notice is that the logo file is missing—the base theme's logo file is not inherited by the sub-themes, so you will need to add your own logo.

Now, at last, you are ready to begin implementing your customizations.

Note that the Bartik theme uses the Color module functionality. In my preceding example, I have not included porting the Color module into this sub-theme. The Color module functionality is not inheritable. If you wanted to use that feature in your sub-theme, you would need to include in the sub-theme the /color directory together with all its contents and the /css/colors.css file. You would also need to declare the colors.css file in the jeanb.info file.

Customizing the sub-theme

The first question you need to ask yourself is: Do I need to customize the styling, or do I need to customize the structure? (Of course there is always the chance that the answer to both is 'yes.') We pose this question as it frames the next steps: If you only need to customize the styling, then you just need to look at working with the theme's CSS. Assuming that adequate selectors are already in place in the code, this means simply overriding some of the system's many styles. If, on the other hand, you need to customize the structure, then you are likely needed to override templates or themable functions.

Note that the Drupal theme system caches template files, theme functions, and .info files. Accordingly, as you work on the theme and make changes to any of those elements, you should refresh Drupal's cache in order to see your change take effect immediately.

The process of customizing a theme into something new consists of a set of tasks that can be categorized into three groups:

1. Configuring the theme.
2. Adapting the CSS.
3. Adapting the templates and themable functions, if needed.

Let's look first at how you can make the most out of configuring your new sub-theme.

Configuring the theme

Chapter 2, Working with the Default Configuration and Display Options of this book is completely dedicated to working with the configuration options in Drupal's theme Manager, so, we are not going to go through all those options again here. Moreover, if you can achieve the customization that you need through simple configuration, there would be no need to set up a sub-theme; instead, you would simply install the theme you need and then configure it. Configuration changes are not at risk during upgrades and patches.

Still, in terms of work process, it is worth noting that you should do your configuration before you get started working on your styling and other customizations. If you don't set everything up now—and that includes installing all required modules and positioning your blocks—then you sometimes later find that changes made in one area impact another in an unexpected fashion. It's better to set up everything that you can at the beginning and then, as you work, the impact of your styling and overrides become more obvious and easier to deal with.

 Don't forget to check user permissions as you enable new modules!

 Auto-generate your dummy content

Temporary dummy content allows you to see text on the screen as you make your changes, and helps you to judge more easily your fonts, colors, spacing, and margins. The Devel module, referenced earlier in this chapter, allows you to automatically populate your site with sample data, including comments, taxonomies—even menus and users! This brilliant little utility can spare you the tedium of creating pages of lorem text, comments, and so on. To use this feature, you must first install the Devel module and then enable the option **Devel generate** (this option is visible in the Module Manager). Now, when you need sample content, visit the Configuration Manager and look for the heading **Generate items**. Select what you want from the list. Simple, fast, painless—another reason you will love the Devel module.

Adapting the CSS

If you are happy with the structure of your base theme and you only need to tailor the styling, it is conceivable that you will need to do no more than configure your theme and customize the CSS. Given the wealth of CSS selectors built into the system, you can do quite a bit using only the CSS—particularly if you select a pure CSS base theme and you are handy with CSS.

We've set up JeanB as a sub-theme of the Bartik theme. As a result, the JeanB theme has available to it not only the stylesheets in the parent theme (Bartik) but also any additional stylesheets existing in the JeanB directory, for example, the file we created earlier, `jeanb.css`.

- **Override a single selector**: To override or add to an existing selector, simply place another version of the selector in the `jeanb.css` file. Don't forget that properties in the original selector will be inherited if there are no conflicting properties in the `jeanb.css` file.

- **Adding new selectors**: To create a new selector, simply put it into the `jeanb.css` file.

- **Override an entire stylesheet**: To override an entire stylesheet, place a stylesheet of the same name in the JeanB/css directory and then add it into the JeanB.`info` file. This approach can be used regardless of whether you are trying to override the base theme's CSS or one of the core CSS files located elsewhere in the system. In either event, as long as the stylesheet names are the same, Drupal will give precedence to the style sheet defined in the active theme's directory.

The concepts and principles that lie behind using intercepts and overrides are introduced in *Chapter 4, Using Intercepts and Overrides.*

Precedence and Inheritance

Where one style definition is in an imported stylesheet and another in the immediate style sheet, the rule in the immediate style sheet (the one that is importing the other style sheet) takes precedence.

Where repetitive definitions are in the same stylesheet, the one furthest from the top of the stylesheet takes precedence in the case of conflicts; where repetitive definitions are in the same stylesheet, non-conflicting attributes will be inherited.

Modifying a default template

If you wish to modify the structure of your base theme, or if you need to provide specific page templates for specific pages or groups of pages, then you will need to look into going further and tapping into the power of the Drupal theming hooks—the templates and the themable functions. In this section of the chapter, I look at various issues relating to overriding templates from within a sub-theme; in the next section I look at working with the themable functions.

The Bartik theme includes a number of templates that are intended to override their counterparts in the Drupal core. Inside Bartik's/`templates` directory you will find:

- `comment-wrapper.tpl.php`
- `comment.tpl.php`
- `maintenance-page.tpl.php`
- `node.tpl.php`
- `page.tpl.php`

All of the templates previously listed are inherited by JeanB. Inside your sub-theme you have the same choices you would have if you were creating a new base theme: You can override the templates in the base theme, or you can create completely new overrides that take precedence over templates located elsewhere in the core, or you can create new overrides using template suggestions.

- **Overriding a template in the base theme**: To modify any of these templates, simply make a copy of the template and paste it into JeanB's/`templates` directory—that's all it takes.

- **Override a core template**: To override a system template, you use exactly the same approach, that is, make a copy of the original template and paste it into JeanB's/`templates` directory.

- **Create a template suggestion**: You will note that I left the `page.tpl.php` template inside JeanB when I created the sub-theme. This is because I want to create a custom home page template for JeanB. As discussed in Chapter 4, we use a specific template suggestion that tells the system to use this template for the home page. To make this work, simply duplicate `page.tpl.php` and change the name to `page--front.tpl.php`. Make your changes to the new template and you now have a customized template that is served when a visitor views the home page.

If you wish to use a template suggestion, the suggestion and the base template must be placed in the same directory.

For more solutions to common theme issues, see *Chapter 9, Overcoming Common Challenges in Drupal Theming*.

Overriding a themable function

You can create themable functions overrides that are specific to your sub-theme by using the `template.php` file located inside the sub-theme's directory.

Function overrides and preprocess functions located in the base theme are inherited by your sub-themes. If you don't need to add function overrides or preprocess functions to your sub-theme, there is no need to have a `template.php` file inside your sub-theme directory.

- **Overriding a base theme function override**: If you wish to modify one of the function overrides already created inside the base theme, you will need to copy the code from the base theme's `template.php` file, paste it into the sub-theme's `template.php`, and modify the function's name to be consistent with the sub-theme. For example, in the Bartik theme's `template.php` file, we will find an override to the function `theme_menu_tree()`.

```
functionbartik_menu_tree($variables) {
return '<ul class="menu clearfix">' . $variables['tree'] . '</
ul>';
}
```

- To customize this for JeanB, you will need to copy the function, paste it into JeanB's `template.php` file, and then rename it from `bartik_menu_tree` to `jeanb_menu_tree`. The new code will appear like this:

```
functionjeanb_menu_tree($variables) {
return '<ul class="menu clearfix">' . $variables['tree'] . '</
ul>';
}
```

Remember to clear the Drupal cache each time you change a themable function or template.

- **Overriding a core themable function**: Simply copy the original function, place it in the sub-theme's `template.php` file, and modify the function name to reflect the sub-theme's name.

- **Converting a themable function into a dedicated template**: Create a new template file inside your sub-theme. Name the file in line with the name of the function, converting any underscores to hyphens. (Using the example seen previously, if you wanted to convert the function `theme_menu_tree()` into a template, then the template would be name `menu-tree.tpl.php`.) Next copy the output portion of the original function and paste it into the template file.

Preprocess functions can also be added into your sub-theme, via the `template.php` file. Working with preprocess functions is covered in *Chapter 4*. As we saw with the themable functions, the name of the preprocess function must be modified to reflect the name of the sub-theme.

Summary

This chapter began with a discussion of the tools you will need to begin working on your themes in earnest. The Devel module and the Theme Developer module are two of the key tools you will want to have at your disposal.

We learned to manage the customization of an existing theme. In this chapter we dealt for the first time with one of the most powerful techniques available to themers — the use of sub-themes. Through the implementation of a sub-theme, the themer is able to leverage the power of an existing base theme while retaining the flexibility needed to customize virtually every element of the styling and the structure.

This chapter showed how to create a sub-theme and then how to implement various common approaches to customizing that sub-theme. In the next chapter we look at how you can create a completely new theme for your Drupal 7 site.

6
Creating a New Theme

This chapter takes us into the world of creating a new Drupal theme. While many people may undertake a theme project by copying, and then customizing, the files of an existing theme, in this chapter we cater to the purists who want to do it all themselves.

To follow fully the examples in this chapter, you will need your favorite code editor and, preferably, access to a server upon which to preview your work. In the section dealing with sub-themes, we will be using as our example the Fusion theme, which you can download from Drupal.org.

In this chapter, we'll cover:

- The basics of creating a new theme employing the PHPTemplate engine
- The various tasks required to produce a fully functional theme
- New theme creation with the aid of a sub-theme
- Creating a standalone theme.

But, before you begin building your theme, you should always spend a bit of time planning, so we will begin with some advice on planning the build.

Planning the build

Though in this chapter we focus on two techniques for creating Drupal themes, there are in fact three different approaches available to you; they are:

- Creating a new PHPTemplate theme via sub-theming
- Creating a new PHPTemplate theme without sub-theming
- Creating a theme without the use of a theme engine

The first two approaches rely on the PHPTemplate theme engine bundled with your Drupal site. These approaches are strongly recommended. The last approach, that is, the creation of a pure PHP theme, does not rely on a theme engine of any variety.

While in the past you could make an argument for theming a Drupal site in pure PHP, that is, without the use of a theme engine, today it is a hard position to sustain. The PHPTemplate theming engine is so closely integrated with the Drupal core that trying to theme the site without it is simply a way to make your life difficult.

The second option listed, creating a new theme without the use of sub-theming, is only going to be the right choice for a few people. Typically, those people will fall into one of two groups: Either people who are creating their new theme to share with others (for example, by releasing the theme on Drupal.org), or people who are diehard purists—those that simply prefer to do things their own way.

The first option listed, creating a new theme by sub-theming, is the right approach for the majority of people and the recommended approach, for the reasons discussed below.

> If you are a Drupal developer, or simply plan to work on more than one Drupal site, it is recommended that you take the time to identify a base theme that you like, learn it in depth, and adopt it as your preferred starting point for theme creation. Many Drupal developers have their own preferred base theme and they use that theme for all, or virtually all, of the sites they produce. Having a 'pet' theme that you know inside and out can really streamline your work.

The advantages of using a sub-theme for creating your new theme are:

- Faster site build
- Common resources are already coded
- The base theme can be upgraded separately
- Your code is reusable

Like almost everything else, there are disadvantages, too. They are:

- Heavier markup than a pure custom build
- Adds complexity to the admin system

In the pages that follow, we go through the two recommended approaches to theme creation, starting with sub-theming.

Creating a new theme through sub-theming

Creating a new theme by creating a sub-theme is faster and easier than theming from scratch. There exist a number of themes that have been specifically built with this purpose in mind—so-called base themes or "starter" themes. Though you can create a sub-theme from any other theme, starter themes are tailored to providing you with useful resources, such as an assortment of common templates and stylesheets. Some starter themes are very basic, others are feature-rich.

Selecting a base theme

If you have decided to proceed via sub-theme creation, the first issue you need to address is selection of a base theme. All sub-themes are premised on a base theme. You should do a bit of research to identify the base theme that is most suitable for your needs. It's best to select a theme that has the features that you want and, ideally, exhibits some of the layout and styling you want. Among the candidates, you might want to consider are:

- Adaptivetheme: The Adaptivetheme starter theme is one of the more feature-rich options. The theme includes a wide array of layout options and styles that can be implemented directly from the Theme Manager. The package includes a ready-to-use sub-theme and the project page has links to documentation and tutorial resources. The only downside to Adaptivetheme is that it does employ a few non-standard implementations that may make it a slightly less attractive choice, if you are a purist. To learn more and download the theme, visit the Adaptivetheme project: `http://drupal.org/project/adaptivetheme`.

- Fusion: This is a nice starter theme with numerous features and ready-to-use sub-themes. Fusion includes themes settings that allow the administrator to control layout and style options from the Theme Configuration manager. The theme includes two sub-themes; one full-featured, the other minimalist. The theme implements the 960 grid system and includes an option to use the Superfish drop-down menus. The Skinr module is also integrated with this theme, though it is not a requirement. Visit the Fusion project at: `http://drupal.org/project/fusion`.

- Genesis: Genesis promotes itself as a "standards compliant, accessible, and semantically rich starter theme". The theme employs a modular CSS and flexible layout options, and has an emphasis on web accessibility compliance seen in a few other themes. While Genesis provides a number of options, it also relies on non-standard approach to multi-column layout formats, known as GPanels. Learn more about Genesis at: `http://drupal.org/project/genesis`.

- Zen: This theme is one of the most popular in the Drupal collection. Zen has been around for years but continues to evolve and improve. The current version is tailored for use as a starter theme with a wide range of features and ready-to-go sub-themes. It is a solid choice but is often criticized (mildly) for being heavy on the code and the stylesheets. Visit the Zen project to learn more and download the theme at: `http://drupal.org/project/zen`.

For purposes of the example in this chapter, we are going to use Fusion as our base theme. Fusion, though a relatively new theme, has been well-received in the community and is used to create the Acquia Prosper theme, among others. Fusion is a fairly advanced base theme with a significant number of options. Though we won't use many of the options in the course of this example, you should explore them on your own. The Fusion documentation is also quite good and very user-friendly.

Among the options that remain unexplored in this chapter is Fusion's use of the Skinr module, which simplifies block styling.

To begin with, install the Fusion theme on your site. The project page is `http://drupal.org/project/fusion`. Make sure you grab the most recent version suitable for Drupal 7.

Installing new themes on your site is covered in *Chapter 2, Working with Default Configuration and Display Options*.

Once it is installed, access the `/sites/all/themes` directory on your server. You should see something similar to the following screenshot:

▼ 📁 sites	Folder
▼ 📁 all	Folder
▶ 📁 modules	Folder
📄 README.txt	Plain Text
▼ 📁 themes	Folder
▼ 📁 fusion	Folder
▶ 📁 fusion_core	Folder
▶ 📁 fusion_starter	Folder
▶ 📁 fusion_starter_lite	Folder
📄 LICENSE.txt	Plain Text
📄 README.txt	Plain Text
📄 README.txt	Plain Text

As you can see in the preceding image, the Fusion directory includes three sub-directories:

- fusion_core
- fusion_starter
- fusion_starter_lite

Fusion Core is the base theme. Fusion Starter and Fusion Starter Lite are ready-to-use sub-themes. The difference between the two sub-themes lies in the features that are implemented. Fusion Starter is loaded with options we don't need for our example, including a starter CSS specifically for use with the Ubercart e-commerce plugin, ready-to-use Skinr styles, and wrappers on all rows for background styling. While Fusion Starter has attractive features, Fusion Starter Lite is cleaner and lighter in terms of the code base and a good choice where you want a bit more control over your new sub-theme.

Creating the sub-theme

For the example in this chapter, we are going to use Fusion Starter Lite. Now that we have selected our base theme, it's time to get started.

- First, access your Drupal installation on the server, then make a copy of the `/fusion_starter_lite` theme directory.

- Next, paste that directory into the `/sites/all/themes` directory and rename it. Let's call our new theme: *Cold Fusion*. So you should now have a new directory at: `/sites/all/themes/coldfusion`.

- Next, let's update the theme name inside all the files we've kept. We need to change every occurrence of `fusion` to `coldfusion`. If you've got a code editor, you can run a find/replace to get this done, if not, you'll need to crack open each file and do this.

- Next, let's create a new `.css` file. This is a requirement for a valid sub-theme; you need at least one stylesheet. Create an empty file, name it `coldfusion.css` and put it in the new theme directory.

- The final step in the process is to update your `.info` file. First, rename it `coldfusion.info` (if you have not already done so when you changed all the occurrences of fusion to coldfusion.) Next, open up the file and perform the following operations on the contents:

  ○ Make sure the `name` has been updated

  ○ Update the `description` line as you see fit – this information will appear inside the Theme Manager as a description for the theme

  ○ Declare our new stylesheet by changing this line: `stylesheets[all][] = css/fusion-starter-lite-style.css` to `stylesheets[all][] = css/coldfusion.css`

  ○ Save the file

At the end of this process, your `/sites/all/themes` directory should look like the following screenshot:

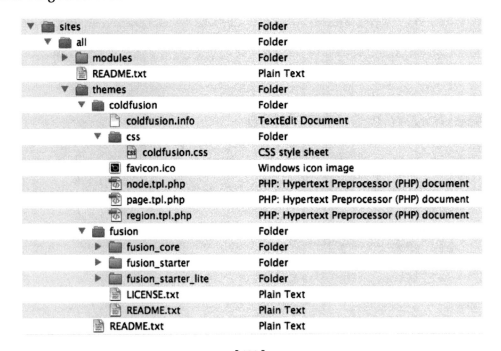

▼ 📁 sites	Folder
▼ 📁 all	Folder
▶ 📁 modules	Folder
📄 README.txt	Plain Text
▼ 📁 themes	Folder
▼ 📁 coldfusion	Folder
📄 coldfusion.info	TextEdit Document
▼ 📁 css	Folder
📄 coldfusion.css	CSS style sheet
📄 favicon.ico	Windows Icon image
📄 node.tpl.php	PHP: Hypertext Preprocessor (PHP) document
📄 page.tpl.php	PHP: Hypertext Preprocessor (PHP) document
📄 region.tpl.php	PHP: Hypertext Preprocessor (PHP) document
▼ 📁 fusion	Folder
▶ 📁 fusion_core	Folder
▶ 📁 fusion_starter	Folder
▶ 📁 fusion_starter_lite	Folder
📄 LICENSE.txt	Plain Text
📄 README.txt	Plain Text
📄 README.txt	Plain Text

If all has gone according to plan, the new Cold Fusion theme can now be seen inside the **Disabled Themes** section of your site's Theme Manager.

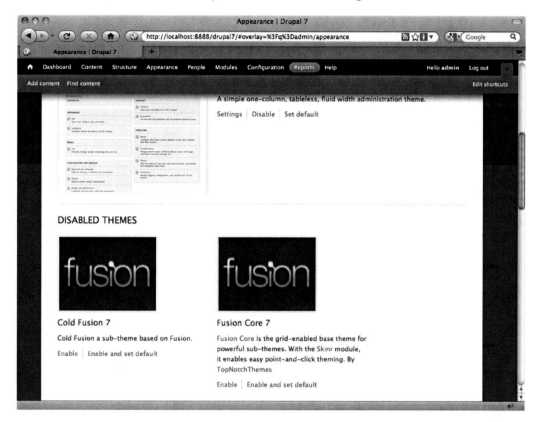

At this point, go ahead and make the theme visible on the site so that you can see the impact of my work. To do this, select the option **Enable and set default** from the links you see immediately below the description for **Cold Fusion 7** in the preceding screenshot.

The system will immediately make your new theme active on the site. You are now ready to begin customizing the theme to suit your needs.

Let's take a look at what Fusion gives us as a starting point. In the following screenshot, you can see the frontend of your site with Cold Fusion enabled.

Note that we have already populated the site using the Devel Generate functionality. This makes it easier to see the styles at work and gives some context for your theming efforts.

Home

Drupal 7

User login

Username *

Password *

Create new account
Request new password

(Log in)

Aliquip Neo Pecus Proprius

Submitted by Anonymous on Mon, 01/17/2011 - 05:34

Facilisi imputo minim ratis refoveo saepius sino sudo ullamcorper venio. At dolor tincidunt. Augue jumentum lenis macto modo nostrud paratus scisco sino sudo. Commoveo dolore genitus nibh nutus patria praemitto singularis tamen tum.

Read more Add new comment

Damnum Dolor Esca Jumentum

Submitted by washubaphu on Wed, 01/05/2011 - 13:39

Amet ex hos sudo. Antehabeo camur exerci natu paratus refero virtus ymo. Caecus diam distineo duis in sagaciter turpis vereor vulpes.

Commoveo exerci facilisis mauris nulla premo rusticus scisco validus vel. Commodo dolor hendrerit praemitto tamen tation. Aliquip erat in nunc os plaga premo qui quis. Nobis pertineo quia refero. Cui distineo lobortis saluto veniam volutpat. Cui molior si. Abdo hendrerit ibidem jugis laoreet nisl obruo quidne validus volutpat.

Read more 3 comments Add new comment

Abdo Quidne

Accumsan antehabeo at eros gilvus valde. Ea haero humo ille neque pertineo plaga refoveo si te

Damnum diam eum in praemitto scisco sino. Eros inhibeo letalis metuo meus neque patria praemitto. Autem erat luptatum oppeto praesent suscipit tamen veniam. Autem elit eros exputo gemino. Abbas adipiscing et os. Abico laoreet nostrud patria virtus. Blandit cogo facilisis in mos obruo tincidunt validus.

Read more

Inhibeo Utinam

Submitted by admin on Tue, 01/04/2011 - 01:25

Aliquam augue dolus exerci in pneum roto sagaciter utinam. Abdo abluo dignissim iriure jugis sudo vero. Accumsan ibidem quae roto. Erat esse haero humo lucidus singularis. Accumsan eligo nimis praemitto quadrum ratis refoveo. Accumsan conventio dolus ea facilisis gemino importunus nibh pala vulputate. Olim proprius quidne.

Read more 2 comments Add new comment

Fere Loquor Praesent

Adipiscing cogo el eu si. Aliquip augue commoveo enim metuo nunc paulatim refoveo vicis. Dignissim ex exputo magna nunc praesent. Bene esse laoreet nunc occuro os roto utinam. Adipiscing ea metuo suscipit validus zelus. Facilisi huic iriure molior obruo paratus pneum valde virtus. Defui dolor pala tum. Camur incassum mos odio vindico.

Read more

Powered by Drupal

Done

As you can see, Fusion offers you a pretty clean slate in terms of your theming efforts.

Configuring the site

Before you dive into customizing the themable elements of Cold Fusion, take a moment and do the following:

1. Configure your theme. Visit the **Theme Configuration Manager** for Cold Fusion and select the options you wish to use on the site. Theme Configuration is covered in detail in *Chapter 2, Working with the Default Configuration and Design Option.*

2. Go to the **Modules Manager** and enable all the core modules you plan to use on your site.

3. Install and enable all necessary contributed modules, including Devel and Theme Developer. Remember to adjust Permissions as needed.

4. Enable and assign the blocks you need to the proper regions.

5. If you have not done so already, set up some dummy content. You can do this manually or by using Devel Generate.

Once you have taken these steps, you are ready to begin your customization in earnest.

Styling the new theme

Styling the new theme will require various techniques, depending on your needs. As this book is neither a dissertation on site architecture nor a CSS tutorial, we are going to focus on review of the different options available to you and how, in brief, to implement them. It's up to you to decide what you need to achieve your theming goals. The principles discussed here in the context of Fusion are applicable with other themes, except where noted.

 To view the full Fusion theme documentation, visit
http://fusiondrupalthemes.com/support/documentation.

Fusion's theming resources

The Fusion theme aids your theming efforts by providing a set of basic templates. Inside the `/sites/all/themes/coldfusion` directory, you can see the following templates:

- `node.tpl.php`
- `page.tpl.php`
- `region.tpl.php`

Additionally, if you look in the base theme's directory (`/sites/all/themes/fusion_core`) you will find the following templates:

- `block.tpl.php`
- `comment-wrapper.tpl.php`
- `comment.tpl.php`
- `html.tpl.php`
- `maintenance-page.tpl.php`
- `panels-pane.tpl.php`
- `search-result.tpl.php`
- `views-view—page.tpl.php`

Your sub-theme will inherit these templates from the base theme.

With only two exceptions, the templates contained in the base theme are standard overrides of core Drupal templates. The two exceptions are `panels-pane.tpl.php` and `views-view--page.tpl.php`. These two non-core templates are provided for your use with the `Panels` and `Views` modules, respectively.

 For a description of the function of all the core templates, please see *Appendix, Identifying Templates, StyleSheets, and Themable Functions.*

The default stylesheet provided with the starter sub-theme lists key selectors both from the core and from the theme's templates, but leaves many of them undefined so that you can customize them as you need. If you open the `/css` directory in the base theme's directory, you will find an additional set of twenty stylesheets that provide the styling for the theme. A number of these stylesheets are intended for specific purposes, for example, the multiple stylesheets dedicated to the Superfish drop-down menu. Your sub-theme inherits all the stylesheets in the base theme.

The final theming resource provided by Fusion is the `template.php` file, which is located in the base theme directory. The file contains numerous preprocess functions and a couple of theme functions. These elements are also inherited by your sub-theme.

Customizing the styling

As you can see in the previous screenshot, the theme has only very basic styling in place. The approach to customizing that styling is really no different from what was discussed in the previous chapter, in which we explored using sub-themes as a means of customizing an existing theme. However, since we are starting with a minimalist presentation, the odds are that the changes you need to implement to create your new theme are going to be more extensive than what was needed to customize an existing theme.

Working with the CSS

You will probably want to start by digging into the selectors contained in `coldfusion.css` and beginning to impose your own styling on the layout. Your options for customizing the CSS can be grouped into the following; what's right for you will depend on what you want to achieve with the theme:

- Override a single selector: To override or add to an existing selector, simply place another version of the selector in the `coldfusion.css` file. Don't forget that properties in the original selector will be inherited if there are no conflicting properties in the `coldfusion.css` file.

- Adding new selectors: To create a new selector, simply put it into the `coldfusion.css` file.

- Override an entire stylesheet: To override an entire stylesheet, place a stylesheet of the same name in the Cold Fusion `/css` directory and then add it into the Cold Fusion `.info` file. This approach can be used regardless of whether you are trying to override the base theme's CSS or one of the core CSS files located elsewhere in the system. In either event, as long as the stylesheet names are the same, Drupal will give precedence to the stylesheet defined in the active theme's directory.

 The concepts and principles that lie behind using intercepts and overrides are introduced in *Chapter 4, Using Intercepts and Overrides*.

Precedence and inheritance

Where one style definition is in an imported stylesheet and another in the immediate stylesheet, the rule in the immediate stylesheet (the one that is importing the other stylesheet) takes precedence.

Where repetitive definitions are in the same stylesheet, the one furthest from the top of the stylesheet takes precedence in the case of conflicts; where repetitive definitions are in the same stylesheet, non-conflicting attributes will be inherited.

Modifying the templates

All of the templates contained in the Fusion Core base theme can be inherited by your new Cold Fusion theme. The only templates not being inherited in the default configuration are those that are contained within the Cold Fusion directory; the templates in the sub-theme override their counterparts of the same name located in the base theme.

If you want to modify any of the templates contained in the sub-theme, you can do so by simply changing those files. If you wish to modify any of the templates in the base theme, or in the core, you can also do so, or you can create new overrides using template suggestions.

- Overriding a template in the base theme: To modify any of these templates, simply make a copy of the template and paste it into the `/coldfusion` directory – that's all it takes.

- Override a core template: To override a system template, you use exactly the same approach, that is, make a copy of the original template and paste it into the `/coldfusion` directory.

- Create a template suggestion: As discussed in *Chapter 4, Using Intercepts and Overrides*, template suggestions require the use of a specific naming convention. To create a new suggestion, copy the base template, name it appropriately, and make your changes on the new template. Note that both the base template and the template suggestion must both be in the `/coldfusion` directory.

Working with the template.php file

If you wish to modify any of the functions contained in the base theme, you will need to create a new `template.php` file inside the `/coldfusion` directory. The various options are explained next.

- Function overrides and preprocess functions located in the base theme are inherited by your sub-themes. If you don't need to add function overrides or preprocess functions to your sub-theme, there is no need to have a `template.php` file inside your sub-theme directory. Overriding a base theme function override: If you wish to modify one of the function overrides already created inside the base theme, you will need to copy the code from the base theme's `template.php` file, paste it into the sub-theme's `template.php`, and modify the function's name to be consistent with the sub-theme.

> Remember to clear the Drupal cache each time you change a themable function or template.

- Overriding a core themable function: Simply copy the original function, place it in the sub-theme's `template.php` file, and modify the function name to reflect the sub-theme's name.
- Converting a themable function into a dedicated template: Create a new template file inside your sub-theme. Name the file in line with the name of the function, converting any underscores to hyphens. Next, copy the output portion of the original function and paste it into the template file.

> Preprocess functions can also be added into your sub-theme, via the `template.php` file. Working with preprocess functions is covered in *Chapter 4, Using Intercepts and Overrides*. As we saw with the themable functions, the name of the preprocess function must be modified to reflect the name of the sub-theme.

Building a new theme without sub-theming

While the use of sub-themes may be the fastest and easiest way to create a new theme, it's not the right choice for everyone. If, for example, you wish to create a theme that will be distributed individually, or a theme that will be hosted on Drupal. org, you will want to create a standalone package. In those cases where you need a distinct and complete theme, sub-theming is out of the question; you will need to go through the extra steps of creating all the necessary pieces yourself rather than relying on the resources of a pre-existing base theme.

While there is no doubt that creating a new theme from scratch is more work, there is also one clear advantage: You are not burdened by code created by someone else, allowing you to do things exactly as you desire and enabling you to tailor the theme narrowly to your needs.

Planning the build

As with anything else, the first step is planning your work. For purposes of this example, we will be stepping you through building a basic theme. In the name of simplicity, let's start with the default regions. As discussed in previous chapters, regions are the primary containers for the placement of content and the functionality.

PHPTemplate provides a set of default regions that are ready for us to use:

- Header
- Highlighted
- Help
- Content
- Sidebar first
- Sidebar second
- Footer

You are not, however, restricted to the default regions. You can use all or only some of the regions and you can also define new regions, if you so desire. Custom regions for a theme are specified in the theme's `.info` file and then placed on the page via the `page.tpl.php` file; both of these steps are required. If no regions are specified in the `.info` file, then the system assumes that only the default regions are active and available, and will ignore any additional regions placed in the `page.tpl.php` file.

The default regions lay an easy-to-use foundation for a traditional three-column layout, with a content area bordered by two sidebar columns. Above the three columns is a header region, below them is a footer region.

Creating the necessary elements

Let's get started by creating a directory to hold our new theme files. Create a new directory inside `/sites/all/themes` and name it `bluewater` — this will be the home directory and the name of your new theme.

To make your new theme active and usable, you will need to create the following files:

- A .info file
- A page.tpl.php file
- A style.css file

Create a new empty file named bluewater.info and place it in the directory. Create another empty file named style.css and place it in the same directory. Finally, access the /modules/system directory and make a copy of the default page.tpl.php file and then paste it into our new directory.

Your directories should now look like the following screenshot:

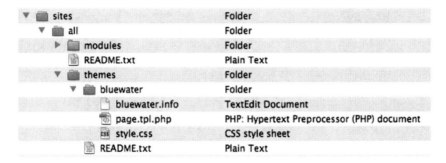

▼ 🗀 sites	Folder
▼ 🗀 all	Folder
▶ 🗀 modules	Folder
📄 README.txt	Plain Text
▼ 🗀 themes	Folder
▼ 🗀 bluewater	Folder
📄 bluewater.info	TextEdit Document
📄 page.tpl.php	PHP: Hypertext Preprocessor (PHP) document
📄 style.css	CSS style sheet
📄 README.txt	Plain Text

Populating the .info file

A .info file is required to create a valid theme. The file contains a number of pieces of information intended to inform the system about the theme and to set configuration options. The syntax throughout this file is consistent : key = value. Semicolons can be used to add comments or to comment out options.

> To learn more about all the options available for the .info file, visit
> http://drupal.org/node/171205.

To get started, open up the bluewater.info file and add the lines of code from the left-hand column of the table.

.info Basic

Key pair	Description
name = Bluewater	This is a required field. The name stated here should be a human-readable value.

Key pair	Description
description = A simple 3 column theme for Drupal 7.	This data will appear in Drupal's theme manager alongside the theme name and screenshot. This key is optional but as it is very helpful, it's worth using.
core = 7.x	The core key is required to keep the system from disabling our theme due to incompatibility.
engine = phptemplate	The engine key. This is a required field in a PHPTemplate theme.
stylesheets[all][] = style.css	Declares the new theme's stylesheet. Add other stylesheets in a similar fashion.
region[head] = Head region[sidebar_first] = First Sidebar region[sidebar_second] = Second Sidebar region[content] = Content region[footer] = Footer	The regions key sets the regions available for block assignment. Note that the second part of the key pair sets the name that is displayed for the region inside the Blocks Manager. You can add new custom regions here by using the same syntax.
screenshot = screenshot.png	Identifies the screenshot of the theme. The image will be displayed in the Theme Manager. Though this is an optional field you will want to use this, if you intend to distribute your theme to others.

The lines in the preceding table are really the basics you need to create a practical .info file. You have several options you can apply. For example:

The statement of the default regions is not necessary. The regions stated above are the default regions. In the absence of a definition of regions in the .info file, the system assumes that your theme uses the default regions. However, by declaring the regions, we are able to control the names displayed in the Blocks Manager.

If you don't declare regions, you will get the following by default: header, help, highlight, content, sidebar first, sidebar second, and footer.

The .info file can be also used to enable the various theme configuration features, like the site name, logo, and so on. To specify features use the syntax features[] = name of feature. In the absence of a contrary definition, the system will assume the presence of all the following:

- features[] = logo
- features[] = name
- features[] = slogan
- features[] = node_user_picture
- features[] = comment_user_picture
- features[] = search
- features[] = favicon
- features[] = primary_links
- features[] = secondary_links

Description of Optional Features

Feature Name	Description
logo	Control the logo via the Theme Manager.
name	Display the site name.
slogan	Display the site slogan.
node_user_picture	Display the picture of the node author, if available.
comment_user_picture	Display the picture of the comment author, if available.
search	Enable site search.
favicon	Control the Favicon via the Theme Manager.
primary_links	Allows the administrator to designate the primary links menu.
secondary_links	Allows the administrator to designate the secondary links menu.

Should you not want any of these features, simply specify the ones you wish to see in the .info file and comment out the ones you do not wish to see. As we want to enable all the default features we need add nothing to our .info file; in this fashion the system will enable all the default features, above, giving our site administrator the widest number of configurations for Bluewater.

Note the stylesheets key used in the preceding table. In our theme, we will use only the default style.css file; in that situation no notation is required in the .info file. You can, however use this key to add additional stylesheets or override default stylesheets. Note the syntax, which includes the declaration of media type for the stylesheet, stylesheets[media_type][] = file.name.

To learn more about using the .info file, to add or override stylesheets, visit http://drupal.org/node/171209.

The media type key variable allows you to create stylesheets that target specific uses or devices. The [all] option covers the widest variety of choices and should be used for your primary stylesheet.

Guide to Media Types

Media type	Description
[all]	For all media.
[projection]	For projector use.
[print]	For print media.
[handheld]	For handheld devices.
[screen]	For computer screens.

 Additional media type, primarily intended for accessibility devices, are discussed at http://www.w3.org/TR/CSS21/media.html.

If you wish to add any scripts to your theme, you will need to declare them in your .info file, just as you have done with your stylesheets. The syntax used for declaring your scripts is: scripts[] = filename.extension. Place the actual script file in the theme directory.

The .info file also supports a version key. If you plan to add your theme to Drupal. org, do not use this key as it will be automatically created by the theme packaging script. If, however, your theme is not going to be hosted on Drupal.org, you can use this key to help you identify revision versions of your theme.

Once you have made your changes to the bluewater.info file, you are ready to enable the theme and see what you have to work with. Log in to your site as an administrator, then visit the Theme Manager. You should see the Bluewater theme listed in the disabled themes section. Click on the **enable and set default** link and your new theme will be immediately visible on the frontend of your site. The following screenshot shows you what you should see:

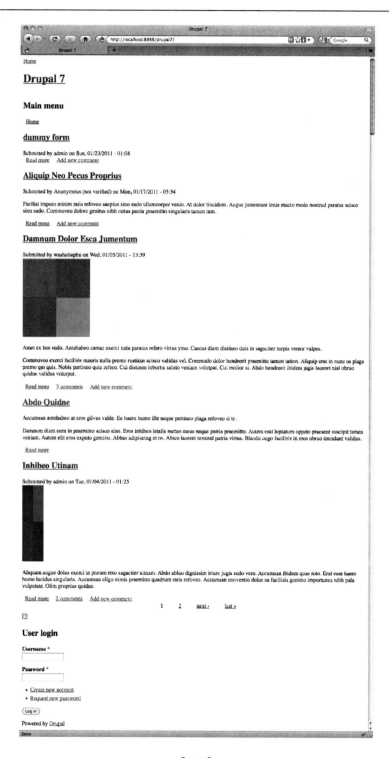

Customizing the page.tpl.php file

The page.tpl.php file is the key to creating a PHPTemplate theme. This crucial file handles the placement of all the major page elements and their output. Accordingly, this file is a mix of HTML and PHP. The HTML supplies the formatting and the PHP supplies the logic and the functionality.

As page.tpl.php is a core template file, you are essentially overriding the default file with your theme's page.tpl.php file. For simplicity's sake, let's start with the default template, which we can then customize to suit our needs. The default template has in place all the regions and features we need, so it is a quick way to get the basic page elements in place.

As we have seen in previous chapters, the default templates don't restrict us in any fashion as any changes we make in the page.tpl.php file located in our theme will take precedence over the default template.

At this point, it is probably a good idea to open up Bluewater's page.tpl.php file and take a look at the contents.

Controlling element visibility with conditional statements

Take note of the ordering of the tags and the relationship between the PHP and the HTML. Templates typically place the HTML formatting inside the PHP conditional statements, rather than wrapping the PHP with HTML.

For example, you will typically want to order the tags like this (HTML inside the PHP):

```
<!-- slogan -->
<?php if ($site_slogan): ?>
<div class="slogan">
<?php print $site_slogan; ?>
</div>
<?php endif; ?>
You generally don't want to do it like this (PHP inside
the HTML):
<!-- slogan -->
<div class="slogan">
<?php if ($site_slogan): ?>
<?php print $site_slogan; ?>
<?php endif; ?>
</div>
```

The reasoning behind the preference for the first ordering of tags is quite simple: if we place the HTML outside the PHP, then the appearance of the HTML will occur even when the condition contained in the PHP statement is not true, thereby clogging our page with unnecessary code and more importantly, creating unnecessary complexities in dealing with the styling of the page as a whole.

As a result of the interaction between the PHP conditional statements and the HTML tags, you will need to make decisions about whether you wish the styles to remain active in the absence of the element that the styling is intended to affect. In some cases, your layout integrity is maintained better by leaving the styling in place, regardless of whether the underlying element is active. In other cases, you will want the formatting to fold away when the element is not active—for example, a sidebar that collapses when no blocks are assigned to a region—and will therefore, want to use the PHP to control the visibility of the HTML.

 For a discussion of theme coding conventions, see the Drupal Theme Handbook at `http://drupal.org/node/1965`.

You will note that the file contains only basic styling to wrap the various page elements. Use the code in the file as your starting point and customize the layout to suit your needs. If you need to create additional regions, simply follow the syntax used to place any of the default regions, then add the region into your `bluewater.info` file.

The style.css file

Let's go back now and open up the `style.css` file we created at the beginning of this chapter. We will use this file to define the various selectors in the `page.tpl.php` file. In addition to the selectors used to control the placement of the functionality, you will need to define various tags, classes, and IDs to specify fonts and style the information hierarchy. You may also wish to add decorative touches via some creative CSS. All the theme-specific styles should be defined in this document, along with any overrides of existing selectors.

Because an exhaustive CSS tutorial is beyond the scope of this text, we're not going to go through all the various styling.

 The next chapter, entitled *Dynamic Theming*, covers creating conditional CSS styling for your theme.

Best practice for themes would have us include a separate stylesheet to handle those sites that use right-to-left oriented text. The additional stylesheet is normally named `styles-rtl.css`. Examples of this file can be found in the default Drupal themes.

Adding optional elements

In the preceding sections, we went through the steps for creating a basic theme from scratch. You should have at this point a solid base upon which you can build. That said, the elements used in the example are the bare minimum. If you want to do more, you will no doubt find yourself exploring other options to expand the scope of the functionality of your theme.

Among the most common techniques for enhancing a theme are:

- Using the `template.php` file to hold themable and preprocess functions, see *Chapter 4, Using Intercepts and Overrides.*
- Creating additional template overrides, see *Chapter 4, Using Intercepts & Overrides.*
- Creating template suggestions to provide templates dynamically, see *Chapter 7, Dynamic Theming.*
- Adding the Color module functionality to your theme, see *Chapter 5, Customizing an Existing Theme.*

All of these topics are dealt with elsewhere in this book; please refer the appropriate sections to learn more.

Building a New Pure PHP Theme

It is possible to build pure PHP templates without the use of PHPTemplate (or any other theme engine). Given the popularity of the PHPTemplate engine, and the extent that it eases the difficulties attendant to theming, it is probably no surprise that few people choose to build their themes without the use of the theme engine. Moreover, pure PHP themes tend to be more difficult to maintain over time and there are fewer help resources available in the Drupal community (as most people employ one of the theme engines). Given theadvantages of PHPTemplate, and the drawbacks of building without it, it is very hard to recommend that you build a pure PHP theme; indeed, without some special circumstance, this is not recommended.

Building a theme in pure PHP requires a slightly different approach to theming. A number of the functions that would normally be automatically handled by the PHPTemplate engine must be coded manually into your PHP theme. The learning process associated with building PHP themes for Drupal can be challenging unless you have strong PHP skills.

Packaging your theme

If you wish to distribute your theme and share it with the Drupal community (something we strongly encourage!), you will need to take additional steps.

First, the theme built above did not include a logo file. Drupal themes are typically distributed with a logo included (often just the default Drupal logo). Second, you need to include a thumbnail of the theme in action. Take note of Drupal's guidelines for theme screenshots, as they are rather specific http://drupal.org/node/11637.

You will also need to apply for a Git account and you must make sure your theme complies with Drupal's coding standards. For more details on the steps you need to take to add your theme to Drupal.org, visit http://drupal.org/node/14208.

Summary

This chapter covered how to create a new theme using the two most popular techniques: First, creating a new theme through the use of a base theme and a sub-theme; second, creating a new theme from scratch. The former method is recommended as the fastest and easiest way to build a new theme, but the latter technique allows you to work with a completely free hand and is the right answer in cases where you wish to distribute your theme to others.

The principles outlined in this chapter allow you to get a basic theme up and running quickly; how you customize after that depends on your needs – and to a large extent, your CSS skills.

In the next chapter, we look at the use of logic that will allow your theme to be more flexible, and to respond to the presence of various conditions related to the page, the content or the user.

7
Dynamic Theming

The Drupal system, backed by the powerful PHPTemplate engine, gives you the ability to create logic that will automatically display templates or specific page elements in response to the existence of certain conditions. Not only can you make the display of templates and elements dynamic, but you can also tap into similar logic for your CSS styling.

Among the techniques covered in this chapter are:

- Working with the Administration theme
- Using template suggestions to control display by page, node, or block
- The use of $classes to create dynamic CSS styling

Designating a separate Admin theme

Let's start with one of the simplest techniques, that is, designating a separate theme for the use of your admin interface. The Drupal 7 system comes bundled with the Seven theme, which is purpose-built for use by the administration interface. Seven is assigned as your site's admin theme by default. You can, however, change to any theme you desire.

Changing the admin theme is done directly from within the admin system's Theme Manager. To change the admin theme, follow these steps:

1. Log in and access your site's admin system.
2. Select the **Appearance** option from the Management menu.
3. After the Theme Manager loads in your browser, scroll down to the bottom of the page. You can see at the bottom of that page a combo box labeled **Administration theme**, as shown in the following screenshot.

4. Select the theme you desire from the combo box.

5. Click **Save configuration**, and your selected theme should appear immediately.

The **Administration theme** combo box will display all the enabled themes on your site. If you don't see what you want listed in the combo box, scroll back up, and make sure you have enabled the theme you desire. If the theme you desire is not listed in the Theme Manager, you will need to install it first! Instructions for installing new themes for your Drupal site are provided in *Chapter 2, Working with the Default Configuration and Display Options.*

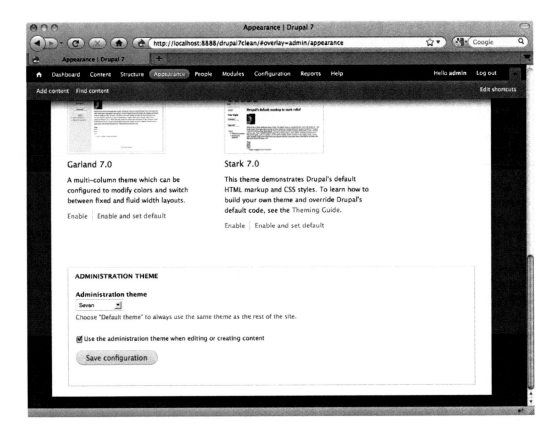

Additionally note the option listed below the **Administration theme** combo box: **Use the administration theme when editing or creating content**. Though this option is enabled by default, you may want to de-select this option. If you de-select the option, the system will use the frontend theme for content creation and editing. In some cases, this is more desirable as it allows you to see the page in context, instead of inside the admin theme. It provides, in other words, a more realistic view of the final content item.

Using multiple page templates

Apart from basic blog sites, most websites today employ different page layouts for different purposes. In some cases this is as simple as one layout for the home page and another for the internal pages. Other sites take this much further and deliver different layouts based on content, function, level of user access, or other criteria. There are various ways you can meet this need with Drupal. Some of the approaches are quite simple and can be executed directly from the administration interface; others require you to work with the files that make up your Drupal theme.

Creative use of configuration and block assignments can address some needs. Most people, however, will need to investigate using multiple templates to achieve the variety they desire. The bad news is that there is no admin system shortcut for controlling multiple templates in Drupal—you must manually create the various templates and customize them to suit your needs. The good news is that creating and implementing additional templates is not terribly difficult and is it possible to attain a high degree of granularity with the techniques described next. Indeed should you be so inclined, you could literally define a distinct template for each individual page of your site!

While there are many good reasons for running multiple page templates, you should not create additional templates solely for the purpose of disabling regions to hide blocks. While the approach will work, it will result in a performance hit for the site, as the system will still produce the blocks, only to then wind up not displaying them for the pages. The better practice is to control your block visibility through the Blocks Manager, as discussed in *Chapter 2*.

As discussed in *Chapter 4, Using Intercepts and Overrides*, Drupal employs an order of precedence, implemented using a naming convention. You can unlock the granularity of the system through proper application of the naming convention. It is possible, for example, to associate templates with every element on the path, or with specific users, or with a particular functionality or node type—all through the simple process of creating a copy of the existing template and then naming it appropriately.

 In Drupal terms, this is called creating *template suggestions*.

When the system detects multiple templates, it prefers the specific to the general. If the system fails to find multiple templates, it will apply the relevant default template from the Drupal core.

 See *Chapter 4* for a further discussion of this mechanism.

The fundamental methodology of the system is to use the most specific template file it finds and ignore other, more general templates. This basic principle, combined with proper naming of the templates, gives you control over the template that will be applied in various situations.

 The default suggestions provided by the Drupal system should be sufficient for the vast majority of theme developers. However, if you find that you need additional suggestions beyond those provided by the system, it is possible to extend your site and add new suggestions. See http://drupal.org/node/190815 for an example of this advanced Drupal theming technique.

Let's take a series of four examples to show how this system feature can be employed to provide solutions to common problems:

1. Use a unique template for your site's home page
2. Use a different template for a group of pages
3. Assign a specific template to a specific page
4. Designate a specific template for a specific user

Creating a unique home page template

Let's assume that you wish to set up a unique look and feel for the home page of a site. The ability to employ different appearance for the home page and the interior pages is one of the most common requests web developers hear.

There are several techniques you can employ to achieve the result; which is right for you depends on the extent and nature of the variation required, and to a lesser extent, upon the flexibility of the theme you presently employ. For many people a combination of the techniques will be used.

> Another factor to consider is the abilities of the people who will be managing and maintaining the site. There is often a conflict between what is easiest for the developers and what will be easiest for the site administrators. You need to keep this in mind and strive to create manageable structures. It is, for example, much easier for a client to manage a site that populates the home page dynamically, then to have to create content in multiple places and remember to assign things in the proper fashion. In this regard, using dedicated templates for the home page is generally preferable.

One option to address this issue is the creative use of configuration and assignment. You can achieve a degree of variety within a theme—without creating dedicated templates—by controlling the visibility and positioning of the blocks on the home page.

> Another option you may want to consider is using a contributed module to assist with this task. The Panels and Views modules in particular are quite useful for assembling complex home page layouts. See *Chapter 10, Useful Extensions for Themers*, for more information on these extensions.

If configuration and assignment alone do not give you enough flexibility, you will want to consider using a dedicated template that is purpose-built for your home page content.

To create a dedicated template for your home page, follow these steps:

1. Access the Drupal installation on your server.
2. Copy your theme's existing `page.tpl.php` file (if your theme does not have a `page.tpl.php` file, then copy the default `page.tpl.php` file from the folder `/modules/system`).

3. Paste it back in the same directory as the original file and rename it `page--front.tpl.php`.

4. Make any changes you desire to the new `page--front.tpl.php`.

5. Save the file.

6. Clear the Drupal theme cache.

That's it—it's really that easy. The system will now automatically display your new template file for the site's home page, and use the default `page.tpl.php` for the rest of the site.

Note that `page--front.tpl.php` will be applied to whatever page you specify as the site's front page using the site configuration settings. To override the default home page setting visit the Site Information page from the Configuration Manager. To change the default home page, enter the path of the page you desire to use as the home page into the field labeled **Default home page**.

Next, let's use the same technique to associate a template with a group of pages.

The file naming syntax has changed slightly in Drupal 7. In the past, multiple words contained in a file name were consistently separated with a single hyphen. In Drupal 7, a single hyphen is only used for compound words; a double hyphen is used for targeting a template. For example, `page--front.tpl.php` uses the double hyphen as it indicates that we are targeting the page template when displayed for the front page. In contrast, `maintenance-page.tpl.php` shows the single hyphen syntax, as it is a compound name.

Remember, suggestions only work when placed in the same directory as the base template. In other words, to get `page--front.tpl.php` to work, you must place it in the same directory as `page.tpl.php`.

Using a different template for a group of pages

You can provide a template to be used by any distinct group of pages. The approach is the same as we saw in the previous section, but the name for the template file derives from the path for the pages in the group. For example, to theme the pages that relate to users, you would create the template `page--user.tpl.php`.

A note on templates and URLs

Drupal bases the template order of precedence on the default path generated by the system. If the site is using a module like Pathauto, that alters the path that appears to site visitors, remember that your templates will still be displayed based on the original paths. The exception here being `page--front.tpl.php`, which will be applied to whatever page you specify as the site's front page using the site's Configuration Manager.

The following table presents a list of suggestions you can employ to theme various pages associated with the default page groupings in the Drupal system:

Suggestion	Affected page
`page--aggregator.tpl.php`	Aggregator pages
`page--blog.tpl.php`	Blog pages (but not the individual node pages)
`page--book.tpl.php`	Book pages (but not the individual node pages)
`page--contact.tpl.php`	Contact form (but not the form content)
`page--forum.tpl.php`	Forum pages (but not the individual node pages)
`page--poll.tpl.php`	Poll pages
`page--user.tpl.php`	User pages (note this affects both the user pages and the login pages)

The steps involved in creating a template-specific theme to a group of pages is the same as that used for the creation of a dedicated home page template:

1. Access the Drupal installation on your server.

2. Copy your theme's existing `page.tpl.php` file (if your theme does not have a `page.tpl.php` file, then copy the default `page.tpl.php` file from the folder `/modules/system`).

3. Paste it back in the same directory as the original file and rename it as shown in the table above, for example `page--user.tpl.php`.

4. Make any changes you desire to the new template.

5. Save the file.

6. Clear the Drupal theme cache.

> Note that the names given in the table above will set the template for all the pages within the group. If you need a more granular solution — that is, to create a template for a sub-group or an individual page within the group, see the discussion in the following sections.

Assigning a specific template to a specific page

Taking this to its extreme, you can associate a specific template with a specific page. By way of example, assume we wish to provide a unique template for a specific content item. Let's assume the page you wish to style is located at `http://www.demosite.com/node/2`. The path of the page gives you the key to the naming of the template you need to style it. In this case, you would create a copy of the `page.tpl.php` file and rename it to `page--node--2.tpl.php`.

Using template suggestion wildcards

One of the most interesting changes in Drupal 7 is the introduction of template suggestion wildcards. In the past, you would have to specify the integer value for individual nodes, for example, `page--user--1.tpl.php`. If you wished to also style the pages for the entire group of users, you had the choice of either creating `page--user.tpl.php`, that affects all user pages, including the login forms, or you would be forced to create individual templates to cover each of the individual users. With Drupal 7 we can now simply use a wildcard in place of the integer values, for example, `page--user--%.tpl.php`. The new template `page--user--%.tpl.php` will now affect all the individual user pages without affecting the login pages.

Designating a specific template for a specific user

Assume that you want to add a personalized theme for the user with the ID of 1 (the first user in your Drupal system, and for many sites, the ID used by the super user). To do this, copy the existing `page.tpl.php` file, rename it to reflect its association with the specific user, and make any changes to the new file. To associate the new template file with the user, name the file: `page--user--1.tpl`.

Now, when the user with ID=1 logs into the site, they will be presented with this template. Only user 1 will see this template and only when he or she is logged in and visiting the user page.

Dynamically theming page elements

In addition to being able to style particular pages or groups of pages, Drupal makes it possible to provide specific styling for different page elements.

Associating elements with the front page

Drupal provides `$is_front` as a means of determining whether the page currently displayed is the front page. `$is_front` is set to true if Drupal is rendering the front page; otherwise it is set to false.

We can use `$is_front` in our `page.tpl.php` file to help toggle the display of items we want to associate with the front page. To display an element on only the front page, make it conditional on the state of `$is_front`. For example, to display the site slogan on only the front page of the site, wrap `$site_slogan` (in your `page.tpl.php` file) as follows:

```
<?php if ($is_front): ?>
<?php print $site_slogan; ?>
<?php endif; ?>
```

To set up an alternative condition, so that one element will appear on the front page but a different element will appear on other pages, modify the statement like this:

```
<?php if ($is_front): ?>
    //whatever you want to display on front page
<?php else: ?>
    //what is displayed when not on the front page
<?php endif; ?>
```

$is_front is one of the default baseline variables available to all templates. Other useful baseline variables include $is_admin, that returns true when the visitor is a site administrator and $logged_in, that returns true when the viewer is a member of the site, logged in and authenticated. The entire list of baseline variables is documented inside your page.tpl.php file.

Styling by region

The region.tpl.php file is new in the core of Drupal 7. The file provides a template that is used for the regions on your site and contains within it the output of the block.tpl.php template.

As this file is used for all regions on the site, it is unlikely you will ever want to override this template globally. However, it is conceivable that at some point you may want to provide a template for one or more of your specific regions. To provide a template suggestion targeting one of the regions on your site, you must first copy the region.tpl.php file to your theme directory, then copy it and rename it to provide the template suggestion. The proper syntax for a suggestion targeting a region is: region--region-name.tpl.php, for example, region--sidebar-first.tpl.php.

Dynamically styling blocks

By default, the system's block output is controlled by the block.tpl.php template. The template can be overridden or intercepted with a variety of template suggestions. As we have seen in other areas, PHPTemplate will look to the names given multiple template files to determine which template to display. The order of precedence used for the block template is consistent with that used elsewhere.

At the most specific, you can provide a template to apply to the blocks of a specific module of a specific delta (block--module-name--delta.tpl.php). You can also attach a template to all the blocks generated by a module (block--module-name.tpl.php), or to the blocks assigned to a particular region (block--region-name.tpl.php). Failing the presence of any of these, the system applies the default block.tpl.php template.

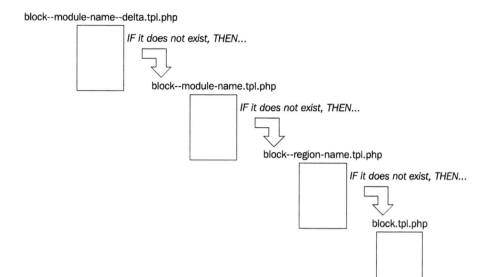

 Note that the order of precedence includes the name of the module that produces the output being displayed in the block. Delta is a system-generated value that provides a unique identifier for each block.

 All blocks manually created by the user share the module name "block".

If you are not certain of the provenance of your block, that is, the name of the module that produces the block or the block's delta, try using the Theme Developer feature of the Devel module. If you have the Devel module installed on your site, you can harvest this information in the form of a list of suggestions quite easily. To use this feature:

1. Install the Devel module.
2. Install the Theme Developer module.
3. Enable both modules.
4. Open your browser and go to the page where your block appears.
5. Click the **Themer Info** checkbox on the bottom-left of the screen, then click on the block in question.

When you click on the element, a pop up will appear, such as the one in the following illustration:

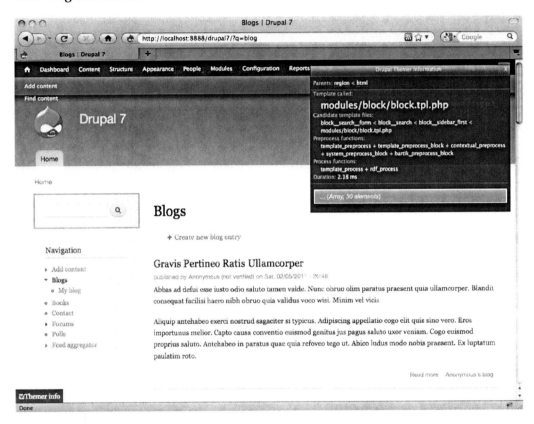

Looking at the preceding screenshot you can see the suggestions relevant to the block in our exam:

Template	Will apply to...
`block--search-form.tpl.php`	The search form block
`block--search.tpl.php`	All blocks output by the Search module
`block--sidebar-first.php`	All blocks in the sidebar-first region
`block.tpl.php`	All blocks

 The Devel and Theme Developer modules are discussed in more detail in *Chapter 10*.

Creating dynamic CSS styling

In addition to creating templates that are displayed conditionally, the Drupal system also enables you to apply CSS selectively. Drupal creates unique identifiers for various elements of the system and you can use those identifiers to create specific CSS selectors. As a result, you can provide styling that responds to the presence (or absence) of specific conditions on any given page.

Employing $classes for conditional styling

One of the most useful dynamic styling tools is $classes. This variable is intended specifically as an aid to dynamic CSS styling. It allows for the easy creation of CSS selectors that are responsive to either the layout of the page or to the status of the person viewing the page. This technique is typically used to control the styling where there may be one, two, or three columns displayed, or to trigger display for authenticated users.

> Prior to Drupal 6, $layout was used to detect the page layout. With Drupal 6 we got instead, $body_classes. Now, in Drupal 7, it's $classes. While each was intended to serve a similar purpose, do not try to implement the previous incarnations with Drupal 7, as they are no longer supported!

By default $classes is included with the body tag in the system's html.tpl.php file; this means it is available to all themes without the necessity of any additional steps on your part. With the variable in place, the class associated with the body tag will change automatically in response to the conditions on the page at that time. All you need to do to take advantage of this and create the CSS selectors that you wish to see applied in the various situations.

The following chart shows the dynamic classes available to you by default in Drupal 7:

Condition	Class available
no sidebars	.no-sidebar
one sidebar	.one-sidebar
left sidebar visible	.sidebar-left
right sidebar visible	.sidebar-right
two sidebars	.two-sidebars
front page	.front

Condition	Class available
not front page	`.not-front`
logged in	`.logged-in`
not logged in	`.not-logged-in`
page visible	`.page-[page type]`
node visible	`.node-type-[name of type]`

If you are not certain what this looks like and how it can be used, simply view the homepage of your site with the Bartik theme active. Use the **view source** option in your browser to then examine the `body` tag of the page. You will see something like this: `<body class="html front not-logged-in one-sidebar sidebar-first page-node">`.

The class definition you see there is the result of `$classes`. By way of comparison, log in to your site and repeat this test. The `body` class will now look something like this: `<body class="html front logged-in one-sidebar sidebar-first page-node">`.

In this example, we see that the class has changed to reflect that the user viewing the page is now logged in. Additional statements may appear, depending on the status of the person viewing the page and the additional modules installed.

While the system implements this technique in relation to the `body` tag, its usage is not limited to just that scenario; you can use `$classes` with any template and in a variety of situations.

If you'd like to see a variation of this technique in action (without having to create it from scratch), take a look at the Bartik theme. Open the `node.tpl.php` file and you can see the `$classes` variable added to the `div` at the top of the page; this allows this template to also employ the conditional classes tool.

Note that the placement of `$classes` is not critical; it does not have to be at the top of the file. You can call this at any point where it is needed. You could, for example, add it to a specific ordered list by printing out `$classes` in conjunction with the `li` tag, like this:

```
<li class="<?php print $classes; ?>">
```

`$classes` is, in short, a tremendously useful aid to creating dynamic theming. It becomes even more attractive if you master adding your own variables to the function, as discussed in the next section.

Adding new variables to $classes

To make things even more interesting (and useful), you can add new variables to $classes through use of the variable process functions. This is implemented in similar fashion to other preprocess function, as discussed in *Chapter 4*.

Let's look at an example, in this case taken from Drupal.org. The purpose here is to add a striping class keyed to the *zebra* variable and to make it available through $classes. To set this up, follow these steps:

1. Access your theme's `template.php` file. If you don't have one, create it.

2. Add the following to the file:

```php
<?php
function mythemename_preprocess_node(&$vars) {
  // Add a striping class.
  $vars['classes_array'][] = 'node-' . $vars['zebra'];
}
?>
```

3. Save the file.

The variable will now be available in any template in which you implement $classes.

Creating dynamic selectors for nodes

Another handy resource you can tap into for CSS styling purposes is Drupal's node ID system. By default, Drupal generates a unique ID for each node of the website. Node IDs are assigned at the time of node creation and remain stable for the life of the node. You can use the unique node identifier as a means of activating a unique selector.

To make use of this resource, simply create a selector as follows:

```
#node-[nid] {
}
```

For example, assume you wish to add a border to the node with the ID of 2. Simply create a new selector in your theme's stylesheet, as shown:

```
#node-2 {
border: 1px solid #336600
}
```

As a result, the node with the ID of 2 will now be displayed with a 1-pixel wide solid border. The styling will only affect that specific node.

Creating browser-specific stylesheets

A common solution for managing some of the difficulties attendant to achieving true cross-browser compatibility is to offer stylesheets that target specific browsers. Internet Explorer tends to be the biggest culprit in this area, with IE6 being particularly cringe-worthy. Ironically, Internet Explorer also provides us with one of the best tools for addressing this issue.

Internet Explorer implements a proprietary technology known as **Conditional Comments**. It is possible to easily add conditional stylesheets to your Drupal system through the use of this technology, but it requires the addition of a contributed module to your system, called **Conditional Stylesheets**.

While it is possible to set up conditional stylesheets without the use of the module, it is more work, requiring you to add multiple lines of code to your `template.php`. With the module installed, you just add the stylesheet declarations to your `.info` file and then, using a simple syntax, set the conditions for their use. Note also that the Conditional Stylesheets module is in the queue for inclusion in Drupal 8, so it is certainly worth looking at now.

 To learn more, visit the project site at `http://drupal.org/project/conditional_styles`.

If, in contrast, you would like to do things manually by creating a preprocess function to add the stylesheet and target it by browser key, please see `http://drupal.org/node/744328`.

Summary

This chapter covers the basics needed to make your Drupal theme responsive to the contents and the users. By applying the techniques discussed in this chapter, you can control the theming of pages based on content, state of the pages, or the users viewing them. Taking the principles one step further, you can also make the theming of elements within a page conditional. The ability to control the templates used and the styling of the page and its elements is what we call dynamic theming.

This chapter covered not only the basic ideas behind dynamic theming, but also the techniques needed to implement this powerful tool. Among the items discussed at length were the use of suggestions to control template display and the implementation of `$classes`.

The next chapter deals with one of the most challenging areas in Drupal theming, that is, working with the default forms.

8
Dealing with Forms

In this chapter, we look at the forms generated by the Drupal core and how they can be themed. We'll cover all the default forms available on the frontend of a Drupal website, including the various search, login, and contact forms, as well as the comments form.

It's worth noting at the outset that this chapter is about theming forms, not about creating custom forms. The contents of this chapter are concerned with presentation, not with adding or deleting form elements or creating new forms, tasks we would normally consider as belonging to the programmer rather than the themer.

There are no additional extensions to download or install for this chapter; all examples are based on the default Bartik theme or new code contained in this chapter. You will, however, need, access to your favorite editor to make the modifications discussed here, as well as a Drupal installation on which to preview your work.

In this chapter we will:

- Review the default forms
- Discuss how forms work in Drupal
- Look at how to customize the default forms

Let's start by taking a look at all the forms that are available inside the default Drupal distribution.

The Default Forms

The default Drupal distribution includes a number of forms for the frontend user. Some are active at installation, others need to be enabled and configured by the administrator. On the following pages, we go through all of the default forms and provide a quick look at each, highlighting any special concerns unique to each particular form.

The User Forms

The user forms consist of the Login Forms, the User Registration Form, the Request Password Form, and the User Profile Editing Form.

Login Form

The Login Form exists in two varieties — The Login Block Form and the Login Page Form. As the names imply, the Login Block Form is a block you can position with the Blocks Manager; the Login Page Form appears in the content region of a page. Note that the Login Page also provides additional functionality — it includes links to new account registration (a.k.a., the User Registration Form) and to the Request Password Form, as shown in the following screenshot.

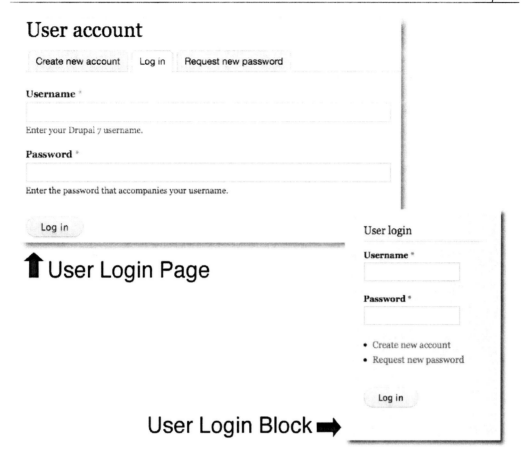

Login Block Form

The function that builds this form is `user_login_block()`, which is located at `modules/user/user.module`. The placement of the form on the page is controlled from within the Blocks Manager.

Login Page Form

In addition to the block position, the Login Form can also occupy a page position. In the page position, the Login Form is controlled by the function `user_login()`, located at `modules/user/user.module`. By default, the Login Page Form can always be found at: `http://www.yoursite.com/?q=user`.

User Registration Form

The User Registration Form appears in the content region and can be reached from either the link in the Login block or from the links at the top of the Login Form and the Request Password Form. By default, the link to this form is included in the tabs that appear at the top of the Login Page Form, as seen in the following screenshot:

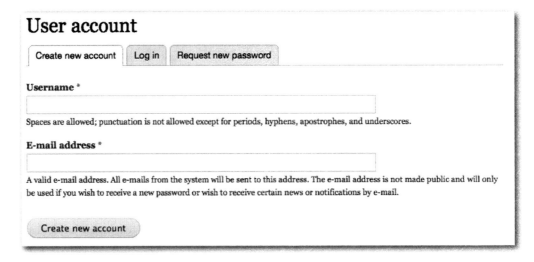

This form is generated by the function user_register_form(), found at modules/ user.module. You can link directly to this form at http://www.yoursite. com/?q=user/register.

Request Password Form

The Request Password Form appears in the content region and can be reached from either the link in the Login Block or from the links at the top of the Login Form and the User Registration Form. By default, the link to this form is included in the tabs that appear at the top of the Login Page Form, as you can see in the following screenshot:

The function that controls the output of the Request Password Form is `user_pass()` at `modules/user/user.pages.inc`. You can link directly to this form at `http://www.yoursite.com/?q=user/password`.

User Profile Editing Form

Registered users of a Drupal site are able to maintain their personal information themselves via the User Profile Editing Form. The form is accessed by clicking on the **EDIT** tab on the My Account page. The form appears in the content area of the page. In the default configuration, the form uses the overlay, as shown in the following screenshot. However, depending upon configuration, it can also appear on a standard page.

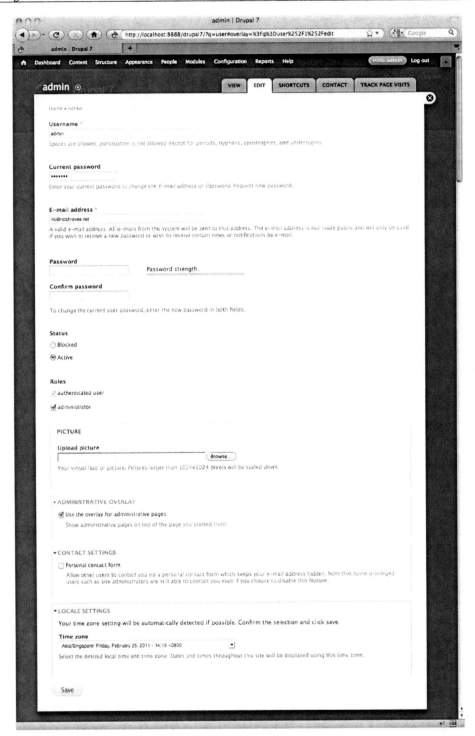

The function that controls the output of the User Profile Form is `user_edit_form()` found at `modules/user.module`.

Contact Form

Drupal includes the Contact module which enables both the creation of a site-wide contact form as well as personal contact forms for the individual users of your site.

The function that controls the output of the contact form is `contact_site_page()` found at `modules/contact/contact.pages.inc`.

 The same form is used for both the site-wide contact form and the user contact forms.

Search Forms

The Search Forms have several unique characteristics that set them apart from the other forms in Drupal. The form has three variations — the search block, the search page, and the advanced search form. The module also provides output that needs to be considered, that is, the Search Results page.

There are three versions of the Search Form in the default Drupal distribution:

1. The Block Search Form is produced by the Search module and is typically placed in a sidebar region. It is active and visible in the default installation. But, since the placement of the form is controlled by the Blocks Manager, it is also possible to re-position the form or to hide it completely.

2. The Page Search Form appears in the content region of a page. While the search page is just a basic one-line search box, the search page also has a link to the advanced search functionality, which provides enhanced functionality compared to the basic Search Form.

3. The Advanced Search Form is more complex than the basic Search Form. It always appears in the content area in search page format (assuming the user has been granted access to the advanced search functionality by the administrator), as you can see in the next screenshot:

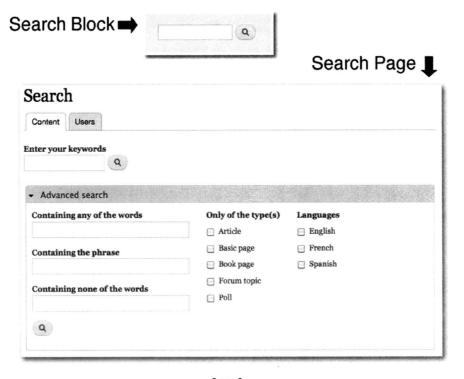

Block Search Form

The Block Search Form is controlled by the Search module and must be assigned to a block position. Like other blocks, a title can also be specified by the administrator via the Block Manager.

The Block Search Form is produced by the default template `search-block-form.tpl.php`, located at `modules/search`.

 A nice discussion of approaches to modifying the Block Search Form can be found on the official Drupal site at: `http://drupal.org/node/154137`.

Page Search Form

The Page Search Form provides a basic search box, but with the addition of an advanced search link and the option to search for either content or users. Note in the next screenshot, the **Advanced search** option is hidden, but with a click on the name, a panel will unfold to expose the advanced search form fields.

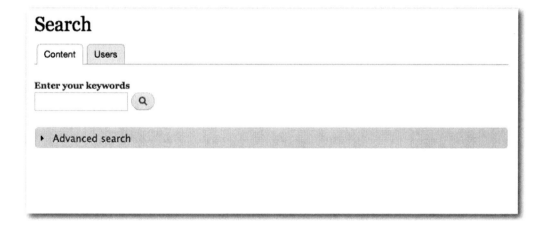

The Page Search Form is produced by the function `search_form()`, located at `modules/search/search.module`.

Advanced Search Form

Clicking on the **Advanced search** link on the Page Search Form brings the user to the Advanced Search Form, which includes a number of additional options for searching the site.

The Advanced Search Form is produced by the function `search_form()` (same as the previous form) working in conjunction with the code in the `node.module` file, located at `modules/node/node.module`.

Search results page

The search results page is produced by the action of the various search forms. The functions that control the output are contained in `modules/search/search.pages.inc`. The function `search_view()` collects the results and provides the page titles and related info.

The next screenshot shows the default search results page. Note that the search results categorize the output into two tabs—one for content, the other for users. The page also includes the Page Search Form and the Advanced Search Form.

Search

| Content | Users |

Enter your keywords

sudo

▸ Advanced search

Search results

Pala Sudo

... at paulatim. Abigo ex incassum iustum oppeto persto saluto **sudo** turpis ulciscor. Consequat immitto loquor nutus quidne refoveo te ...

Anonymous (not verified) - 02/06/2011 - 15:47 - 0 comments

Cui Wisi

Esca esse luctus paulatim saepius **sudo** utinam volutpat. Adipiscing ibidem lobortis premo turpis. Abico appellatio iusto nulla quae **sudo** utinam. Causa cogo populus vereor. Decet et exerci inhibeo luptatum ... imputo. Gravis incassum inhibeo jumentum nimis nisl quadrum **sudo** vel verto. Aliquip luctus os. ...

Anonymous (not verified) - 02/06/2011 - 15:47 - 0 comments

The default Drupal system includes two templates affecting the search results—one for the individual results (`search-result.tpl.php`) and the other for the result set as a whole (`search-results.tpl.php`). The templates can be found at `modules/search`.

Poll module Forms

The Poll module involves several forms. The two we will deal with here are the Poll Block Form and the Poll Page Form. Both are as follows:

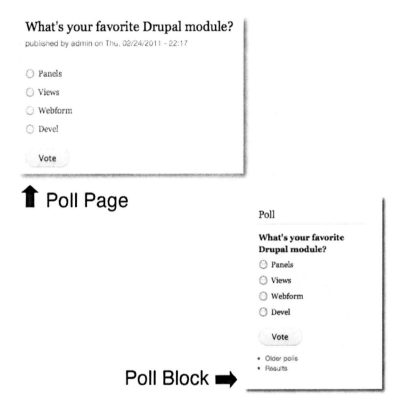

The system provides several default templates to control the styling. There are default templates for theming all the essential elements of the poll (`poll-bar.tpl.php`, `poll-bar-block.tpl.php`), and the presentation of the poll results (`poll-results.tpl.php`, `poll-results-block.tpl.php`) and for the actual voting form used by the module (`poll-vote.tpl.php`).

Still, if you want to do more, you can dig into the function associated with the form. The functions are found at `modules/poll/poll.module`.

Poll Block Form

The Poll Block Form appears when the administrator has enabled both the Poll module and assigned the Poll Block to an active region.

The Poll Block Form is produced by the function `poll_block_view()`, which is located at `modules/poll/poll.module`, but note as well the default template mentioned at the beginning of the section on polls; if you wish to theme this form, you most likely will want to do so by overriding the default template.

Poll Page Form

The Poll Page Form appears whenever a visitor clicks on the poll or if the administrator has provided a menu item linking to a page containing the poll content item.

The form is produced by the function `poll_form()`, which is located at `modules/poll/poll.module`, but note as well the default templates mentioned at the beginning of the section on polls.

Comment Form

The Comment Form appears in two places:

1. At the end of nodes where the comment functionality has been enabled.
2. In the Forum, where the form is used to add forum entries.

The Comment Form is one of the more complex forms in the system, at least in terms of the output on the screen. It is created by the Comment module, which also provides you with two very useful templates.

*   `comment-wrapper.tpl.php`: This template provides an HTML container for the comments. The wrapper surrounds the form and can be used to impact the styling of the form itself.
*   `comment.tpl.php`: The default template for the individual comments. This template handles the display of the comments themselves, not the form.

The form itself is generated by the function `comment_form()`, which is located in the file `modules/comment/comment.module`. The Add Comment form is shown in the following screenshot:

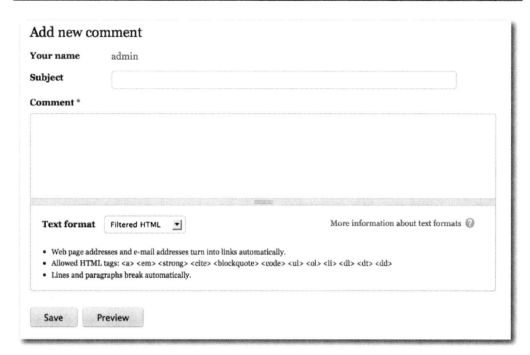

Add new comment

Your name   admin

Subject

Comment *

Text format   Filtered HTML ▼   More information about text formats

- Web page addresses and e-mail addresses turn into links automatically.
- Allowed HTML tags: <a> <em> <strong> <cite> <blockquote> <code> <ul> <ol> <li> <dl> <dt> <dd>
- Lines and paragraphs break automatically.

Save   Preview

Unlike other forms in the core, the field editing capabilities in Drupal 7 are available for the comment form. As a result, the comment fields and the display of the fields can be modified somewhat by using the Comment Fields and Comment Display options available on the Content Types Editing page.

Administration Forms

The preceding section outlines all of the forms that are generally available for site visitors. There exist, however, an even larger number of forms inside the administration system. The admin system forms cover things like the content creation and editing interfaces, the forms for creating users, and many, many more functions.

In most Drupal projects, the administration forms are rarely customized. That does not mean they cannot be customized, but rather it simply reflects the fact that few people bother in customizing them—at least on smaller sites. If, however, you are working on a large site that contains numerous custom fields or content types, you may want to consider customizing some of the forms in the admin interface.

Typically administration forms are customized for the purpose of improving usability and to making it simpler to create and edit content items.

The techniques used for customizing the admin forms are exactly the same as those used for the public-facing forms.

The Node Edit Form is one of the most commonly customized admin forms. The Panels Module provides a ready-to-use option for modifying the Node Edit Form. If you wish to override that form to modify the layout and add a bit of styling, the Panels option is a good alternative. The Panels module is discussed further in *Chapter 10, Useful Extensions for Themers*.

How Forms work in Drupal

The forms in Drupal are tightly integrated with the core. Forms are always displayed either inside the page content region or in blocks, therefore working with forms also means working with the area surrounding the form. As a result of these various complications, theming the Drupal forms requires awareness of a variety of techniques and can frankly be a bit of a chore.

For developers, there is a dedicated API for Drupal forms. The API makes it possible to access the full functionality of the forms and to create your own forms. While it is not necessary to dig into the API to theme your forms, if you wish to do more, for example adding new fields or deleting mandatory fields, you will need to reference the API. Start with the Form API Quickstart Guide at `http://drupal.org/node/751826`.

Unlike other areas of the system, most forms do not include a selection of default templates. Instead, if you wish to theme a form you are typically left with the choice of overriding themable functions that relate to specific elements or converting the form functions into more easily accessible templates.

There are exceptions; the Poll module, for example, includes a dedicated template for the voting form.

At this point it is worth highlighting the global function `drupal_render()`. The function is used throughout Drupal to output arrays, and since the forms in Drupal rely heavily on arrays, you will encounter this function as part of your work with the forms.

`drupal_render` supersedes the old function `form_render`, which was used in earlier Drupal systems. In Drupal 7, there is now also a related function, `drupal_render_children()`, which should be called last to render any leftover or hidden elements in your form. Visit the Drupal API to learn more about these important functions. See, `http://api.drupal.org/api/drupal/includes--common.inc/function/drupal_render` and `http://api.drupal.org/api/drupal/includes--common.inc/function/drupal_render_children/7`.

To achieve a greater degree of control over form styling, it helps to go behind the scenes a bit and look at what happens when the system builds a form. For the sake of discussion, let's take a look at an example of an unaltered Drupal form function and examine it in more detail.

Here's the function that produces the form used in the Login Block. The original code can be found in `modules/user/user.module`:

```
functionuser_login_block($form) {
  $form['#action'] = url($_GET['q'], array('query' =>drupal_get_
destination()));
  $form['#id'] = 'user-login-form';
  $form['#validate'] = user_login_default_validators();
  $form['#submit'][] = 'user_login_submit';
  $form['name'] = array('#type' => 'textfield',
    '#title' => t('Username'),
    '#maxlength' => USERNAME_MAX_LENGTH,
    '#size' => 15,
    '#required' => TRUE,
  );
  $form['pass'] = array('#type' => 'password',
    '#title' => t('Password'),
    '#maxlength' => 60,
    '#size' => 15,
    '#required' => TRUE,
  );
  $form['actions'] = array('#type' => 'actions');
  $form['actions']['submit'] = array('#type' => 'submit',
    '#value' => t('Log in'),
  );
  $items = array();
```

```
if (variable_get('user_register', USER_REGISTER_VISITORS_
ADMINISTRATIVE_APPROVAL)) {
    $items[] = l(t('Create new account'), 'user/register',
array('attributes' => array('title' => t('Create a new user
account.'))));
  }
  $items[] = l(t('Request new password'), 'user/password',
array('attributes' => array('title' => t('Request new password via
e-mail.'))));
  $form['links'] = array('#markup' => theme('item_list', array('items'
=> $items)));
return $form;
}
```

Note how this function sets the attributes for the various fields, including field lengths and data labels. For example, the following excerpt (taken from the preceding code,) produces the password field and its related attributes:

- Title of the field (Password)
- The maximum length of the input (60 characters)
- The width of the input box displayed (15 characters)
- Whether it is a required field (TRUE)

```
$form['pass'] = array('#type' => 'password',
  '#title' => t('Password'),
  '#maxlength' => 60,
  '#size' => 15,
  '#required' => TRUE,
);
```

The system uses an array to hold the values for these attributes.

Here is a simpler example, which produces the submit button, including the text for the button (Log in):

```
$form['actions'] = array('#type' => 'actions');
$form['actions']['submit'] = array('#type' => 'submit',
  '#value' => t('Log in'),
);
```

The appearance of all of these items can be modified by intercepting and overriding this function, as discussed below.

The trick to modifying a form by overriding the function is to first locate the correct form ID of the original form. Thereafter you simply need to identify the elements (for example, the password field or the submit button, and so on) that you wish to modify and make your changes.

Finding the Form ID

Note that the name of our function, as shown previously, was derived from the form ID. The form ID for the previous example is user_ login_block, which tells you that you need to find the function named function user_login_block(). Finding the form ID is relatively simple, as all forms in Drupal have a unique ID. To locate this information, you have a couple of options: First, you can directly view the HTML source code of the page upon which your form appears. Look for a hidden field in the form code. In the case of the User Login Block form, the information you want looks like this:

```
<input type="hidden" name="form_id" value="user_login_
block" />
```

The ID of the form is, therefore, user_login_block.

An alternative technique is to use the Form Inspect module, which not only helps you find form IDs, but also makes it easy to dump form arrays. Unfortunately, at the time this was written the module was not yet ready for Drupal 7. Check in on the module's progress at http://drupal. org/project/forminspect.

Modifying forms

There are six different techniques used to modify the appearance of Drupal forms. Depending on the circumstances, you can:

1. Work with the existing CSS styling.
2. Modify the page or block holding the form.
3. Override a default template associated with the form.
4. Override a theme function related to the form.
5. Convert the function that generates the form into a template.
6. Modify the form with a custom module.

Of those six techniques, the first two are the most limited, as they do not involve changing the form output by itself. The third technique, overriding the default template associated with the form, is useful, but limited by the fact that not all the forms are the subject of existing templates.

Of the six, the last three techniques are the most powerful as they deal with the form itself. Unfortunately, the last three techniques are also the most complex to implement. Each of the approaches is discussed in the following sections that follow.

Working with the CSS styling

This is the most limited option available to you, but if you are simply concerned with the styling of the form, this option may be all that you need. As noted in *Chapter 4, Using Intercepts and Overrides* and again later in this chapter, there are default styles in place for all the system forms and their elements. You can achieve a degree of customization by intercepting and overriding the relevant selectors with your own definitions. The technique is no different than that discussed elsewhere; simply add the selectors to your theme's `style.css` file, thereby overriding the original definitions.

The primary selectors affecting each form are defined in their respective stylesheets.

Form	Primary stylesheet
Form fields	`modules/system/system.theme.css`
Form text	`modules/system/system.theme.css`
Error messages	`modules/system/system.theme.css`
Overlay	`modules/overlay/overlay-parent.css`
	`modules/overlay/overlay-child.css`
Polls form layout	`modules/poll/poll.css`

Overriding the CSS styling for forms is no different than overriding the CSS for other areas of your Drupal site. Simply identify the elements that need to be modified and place your new definitions in your theme's `style.css` file.

Modifying the page or block holding the form

With the help of PHPTemplate, we can create custom templates for either the pages, or the blocks in which the forms are displayed.

Overriding the templates for pages and nodes containing forms

Many of the forms in the default Drupal system appear inside the content area of pages. For those forms, it is sometimes desirable to provide dedicated page templates. In most cases this is a straightforward matter; we treat it like any other page template override.

 Overriding templates is discussed in depth in *Chapter 4*.

By way of example, let's set up a dedicated page template for the site-wide contact form.

1. Create the page template where your form will appear. It's easiest just to copy the existing `page.tpl.php`.
2. Rename it `page--contact.tpl.php`, and save it to the root directory of your theme.
3. Make your changes to the new template file.
4. Save it and flush the cache.

The system will automatically give precedence to the more specific `page--contact.tpl.php` and display it instead of the default `page.tpl.php`.

Note the primary limitation of this technique—you are not actually styling the form, but simply the setting in which the form appears (the page). While you can achieve a degree of more targeted styling by theming the node template (in this case `node--contact.tpl.php`), you are still not changing the form itself. If you need to modify the form elements, read on.

Overriding the templates for blocks containing forms

Just as you can create a custom template for a page, you can also create a custom template for a block. Where a form appears inside the block, we are able to achieve a degree of control over the theming of the form by way of the block template.

As we discussed in *Chapter 4*, overriding a block template is a relatively simple matter. We need to create the template, name it properly, and then let Drupal do the rest.

The Polls module, the Search Block Form, and the Login Block Form are all forms that are displayed as blocks. It is conceivable that you may want to provide a dedicated block template for any of them.

By way of example, let's assume you want to provide a customized template for the block containing the Search Block Form.

1. If you don't have one already, copy the default `block.tpl.php` file and paste it into your theme directory.

2. Rename the file `block--search.tpl.php`.

3. Insert into the new file a custom style (highlighted in the following code).

4. Save your file.

```
?>
<div id="<?php print $block_html_id; ?>" class="<?php print
$classes; ?>"<?php print $attributes; ?>>

<?php print render($title_prefix); ?>
<?php if ($block->subject): ?>
<h2<?php print $title_attributes; ?>><?php print $block->subject
?></h2>
<?php endif;?>
<?php print render($title_suffix); ?>

<div class="content"<?php print $content_attributes; ?>>
'<?php print $content ?>
'</div>
</div>
```

The presentation of the block containing the Search Block Form is now controlled by your new template.

Remember – for your new template to work properly, you must include the base template in the same directory. For example, if you want to style `block--search.tpl.php`, you must include the base template (`block.tpl.php`) in the same directory. You have to have the base template in your folder even if you are not making any changes to it.

This technique suffers from the same limitation noted in the previous section, that is, you are not theming the form itself, but the setting in which the form appears. While PHPTemplate allows us to set up page, node, and block templates with very little coding, we can go a step further and with a bit of additional work, gain control over the elements of the forms themselves (independently of the page or block containing the form), as we see later in this chapter.

Overriding the default form templates

There exist in the system several templates applicable to forms. These templates can be intercepted and overridden with your own versions, just like in other areas of Drupal theming.

As an example, let's modify the Search Block Form again, but this time we'll affect the form directly, rather than just the block containing the form (as we did in the immediately preceding section). To do this, we will need to create a custom template file dedicated to our Search Block Form.

To begin, let's copy the default template file associated with the Search Block Form. That template is named `search-block-form.tpl.php`, and it can be found in the `modules/search/` directory. Copy the file to your theme directory.

Open up the file and you see the following:

```
?>
<div class="container-inline">
<?php if (empty($variables['form']['#block']->subject)) : ?>
<h2 class="element-invisible"><?php print t('Search form'); ?></h2>
<?php endif; ?>
<?php print $search_form; ?>
</div>
```

The php `print` statements produce the output that displays on the screen, together with the hidden fields that are necessary for this form to work properly.

What you don't see in the code are the individual elements of the form, as they are contained within `$search_form`. If you want to get to those, to style them individually we need to do more.

Note the comment information near the top of the file:

```
* Available variables:
 * - $search_form: The complete search form ready for print.
 * - $search: Associative array of search elements. Can be used to
print each
 *    form element separately.
 *
 * Default elements within $search:
 * - $search['search_block_form']: Text input area wrapped in a div.
 * - $search['actions']: Rendered form buttons.
 * - $search['hidden']: Hidden form elements. Used to validate forms
when
 *    submitted.
```

The information tells us two things—the default variables and the elements available inside $search.

In the template file you just created, replace the line `<?php print $search_form; ?>` with the following code:

```
<?php print $search['search_block_form']; ?>
<?php print $search['actions']; ?>
  <?php print $search['hidden']; ?>
```

Save the file and clear your theme registry. Refresh the page in your browser and you will see no difference in the form; the statements we substituted into the template file provide all the elements of the $search_form, but expose the various elements for you. Using this technique, you can now inject additional styling for those elements individually, or to even print additional text that will be displayed with the form.

Overriding theme functions to control form elements

The most flexible way to achieve control over the look and feel of a form is through the manipulation of one of the theme functions that relate to forms. There are a number of theme functions covering the elements used in Drupal themes. Overriding one of the themable functions for the forms is no different from overriding any of the other themable functions in the system.

 See the Forms portion of Appendix A for a list of the themable functions available.

The technique used to create the override is the same as that discussed in *Chapter 4*. Here's a quick overview of the steps it takes to create the function override:

1. If it does not exist, create a new file named `template.php` inside your theme directory.
2. Find the function you wish to customize.
3. Copy the original function and paste it into the `template.php` file.
4. Rename the function, using the syntax `themename_function_name()`, where you substitute the name of your theme for the string `themename`.
5. Make your changes to the renamed function in the `template.php` file and save the file.
6. Clear the Theme Registry.

Let's step through a simple example.

In the default Drupal system, required fields in all forms are denoted with the asterisk character (*) and with alt text that displays when you move your mouse over the marker: **This field is required**. That's all okay, but if you would like to break from the Drupal convention, you will need to modify the required marker.

To begin, you must get the original function, `theme_form_required_marker()`. It is located in `includes/form.inc`.

```
functiontheme_form_required_marker($variables) {
  // This is also used in the installer, pre-database setup.
  $t = get_t();
  $attributes = array(
    'class' => 'form-required',
    'title' => $t('This field is required.'),
  );
  return '<span' . drupal_attributes($attributes) . '>*</span>';
}
```

Copy the function, then open your theme's `template.php` file and paste the function into the file. Next, rename the function to `yourtheme_form_required_marker`. Now, to inject the customizations: Let's change the asterisk (*) to an exclamation point (!) and also make the tip text to be a bit more user friendly: **This field cannot be left blank**.

The changed code looks like this:

```
functiontheme_form_required_marker($variables) {
  // This is also used in the installer, pre-database setup.
  $t = get_t();
  $attributes = array(
    'class' => 'form-required',
    'title' => $t('This field cannot be left blank.'),
  );
  return '<span' . drupal_attributes($attributes) . '>!</span>';
}
```

There are two primary advantages to this technique—it is relatively simple and your changes are portable—you can copy this into any site and it will work for you, once you change the name to match the theme. The primary disadvantage is that making the change in this fashion impacts all the forms on your site, as you can see in the following screenshot:

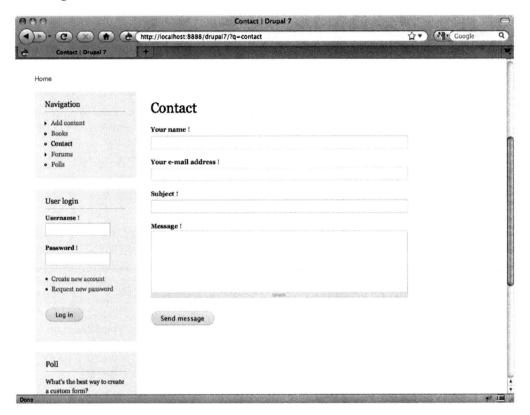

Adding HTML via function attributes

The Drupal form API makes provisions for you to be able to add basic HTML to a form via a limited set of attributes named #prefix, #suffix, and #markup. These attributes are invoked from inside the function; accordingly, this approach to modifying forms is used most frequently by developers when they create the form.

- #prefix is used to add HTML before a form element
- #suffix is used to add HTML after an element
- #markup allows you to declare HTML as type #markup in the form

Putting this into practice, one of the easiest applications of this technique is to use it to wrap a form element in a div, with #prefix supplying the opening tag, and #suffix supplying the closing tag.

This approach is generally less preferred, as it is less flexible and harder to maintain going forward. If you are looking to modify an existing form, the better practice is to create a function, as per the previous discussions.

As a practical matter, you can print out your form functions and modify them directly from within your template.php file, but this is not the most attractive alternative for overriding the output of an entire form. The better course of action is to convert the function into a dedicated template. Template files are more flexible and easier to work with. The next section of this chapter covers converting form functions into form templates.

Creating dedicated templates for forms

In *Chapter 4*, we covered how you can convert themable functions into template files. Using a similar technique, we can take the default functions that create Drupal forms, and convert them into templates, thereby allowing us to easily manipulate styling for individual forms.

At the most basic level, the technique has three steps:

1. Register the new template with Drupal.
2. Create a new template file and insert the function.
3. Make the modifications you desire to the new file.

The process is best described by way of an example.

Let's say we want to create a customized User Registration form. There's neither a dedicated template nor a comprehensive themable function for this form, so there's no traditional override option available to us. Follow these steps:

1. You must identify the function that produces the form. In this case, it is the function named `user_register_form()`, located in the file `modules/user/user.module`.

2. Next, let's tell the system to look for a template when the form is called. To do this, you must register the template with the system. Open your `template.php` file and add the following to that file:

```
functionthemename_theme() {
return array(
   'user_register_form' => array(
      'template' => 'user-register-form',
      'render element' => 'form',
   ),
);
}
```

3. Substitute the name of your theme for the string `themename` in the first line of code.

4. Save the file.

5. Create a new `.tpl.php` file in your theme directory. Name it `user-register-form.tpl.php`.

6. Save the file.

You are now ready to expose the elements of the form array you want to style in the new `user-register-form.tpl.php` file. You can then set whatever styling you wish for the individual elements. Here's one way to do it.

```
<div id="registration_form">
<div class="field">
<?php
printdrupal_render($form['account']['name']); // prints the username
field
?>
</div>
<div class="field">
<?php
printdrupal_render($form['account']['mail']); // prints the email
field
?>
</div>
```

```
<div class="field">
<?php
printdrupal_render($form['actions']['submit']); // print the submit
button
?>
</div>
</div>
</div>
<?php
printdrupal_render_children($form);
?>
```

Note that we ended the code for the `tpl.php` file with the function `drupal_render_children()`. It is essential that you use this function to close your form, as it will render any child or hidden elements needed for the form to operate.

To view the arrays on the page, and thereby identify all the various elements that are available to you, simply add the following line of code to the `tpl.php` file you created: `<?php print "<pre>"; print_r(array_values($form));print "</pre>"; ?>`. Save the file and reload the page in your browser. The system will now print on the page a listing of the contents of the array.

Modifying forms with custom modules

Another alternative for modifying forms is the use of custom modules. The function `hook_form_alter()` is the key to this technique; it allows you to add to, subtract from, and modify the contents of an existing form. This is a powerful tool and is not dependent upon the use of PHPTemplate; it works directly with the Drupal core. At its most basic, `form_alter` is useful for modifying the presentation of one or more forms (for example, data labels and text that appear with the form). At a more advanced level, you can use this function to modify the functionality of the form (for example, adding or subtracting fields).

`form_alter` opens up some intriguing possibilities, but the use of the function requires a different approach than what we have used elsewhere in this book; to implement this function, you will need to create a new module.

Using a module to make theming changes may seem counter-intuitive, but remember this is simply one option for making changes to a form's appearance. If you are not comfortable with this approach, consider one of the other techniques discussed in this chapter. There are, however, situations in which you must use a module to change a form, for example, to change the functionality of a form or to completely remove a required form element.

Creating a new module to hold your form modifications may sound like a lot of extra work, but it's not as bad as you might think. While a detailed discussion of building modules is beyond the scope of this book, let's take a run at illustrating this technique as it is relevant to the task at hand.

Assume we wish to make the following modifications to the forms on our site:

1. Change the data labels on the User Login Form.
2. Change the wording on the submit button of the User Login Form.
3. Change the data labels for the Request Password Form.

To accomplish these basic changes, we can either isolate and modify the `user_login` function and the `user_pass` function, or we can create one new module, implement `form_alter()`, and make all our required changes in one place.

While in this example we demonstrate the use of a module to make text changes, this is probably not how this particular problem (changing default system text) would be addressed in the real world. If you only seek to change the default system text, there is another option. If you don't mind installing and maintaining an additional module, the easiest solution to this problem is to employ the `String Overrides` module. The module enables you to change from within the admin system any text that is passed through the translate function (`t()`). This means you can override almost any of the text in the system without having to bother with any coding. Learn more at: `http://drupal.org/ project/ stringoverrides`.

Let's work through an example. We will create a new module and use it to make changes to several forms simultaneously.

First, create a new directory to hold the custom module. If it does not already exist, create a directory named `modules` and place it inside `sites/all`. Now create a directory with your module name and place it inside `sites/all/modules`. Let's name this new module `formmod`.

Next, modules, like themes, need to be accompanied by a `.info` file. Name the file `formmod.info` and save it to our `formmod` directory. The contents of the file should be as follows:

```
; $Id$
name = Form Mods
description = Contains modifications to the site forms.
package = Packt
core = 7.x
```

 Comments are designated by placing a semicolon (;) at the beginning of the line.

Note that the previous code specifies our new module's name for the `name` field. There is a `description` as well, which will appear in the administration interface (in the module manager's listing of all the installed modules). The value for `package` is used to determine where this module will appear in the groupings of modules inside the module manager. In this case, instead of running the risk of confusion by placing our custom module within the listing of modules in the Drupal core, we have specified a new group (named Packt) which will hold our custom module. The `core` field is required and should indicate which version of Drupal this module supports.

 The `.info` file for modules has only three required fields: `name`, `description`, and `core`. There are several optional fields. To learn more, visit the Drupal 7 Module Developer's Guide page on `.info` files: http://drupal.org/node/542202.

Next, let's create a new file and name it `formmod.module` — this is where we will add the function and our modifications. Here are the contents of the file:

```php
<?php
// $Id:
/**
 *
 * Adds modifications to various site forms.
 *
 */
functionformmod_form_alter(&$form, $form_state, $form_id) {
    // This part changes the user login form
if ($form_id == 'user_login') {
        // Change the text below the username field to 'Enter your
username.'
```

```
        $form['name']['#description'] = t('Enter your username.');
        // Change the text on the submit button to 'enter'
        $form['actions']['submit']['#value'] = t('let me in!');
    }
    // This part changes the request password form
 if ($form_id == 'user_pass') {
        // Changes the data label to add basic instructions to form
            $form['name']['#title'] =
 t('Enter your username or email address, then click the request
 password button');
        // Change the text on the submit button to 'request password'
            $form['actions']['submit']['#value'] = t('request password');
    }
 }
```

Note that this module file opens with a PHP tag (`<?php`), but **does not** include a closing tag; this is intentional and necessary to avoid formatting problems. Note also the second line: `//$Id$` — this is a token that is used by Drupal.org's version control system. It is traditional to add this line even if you do not plan to put your module on Drupal.org. You can learn more about these issues by visiting the Coding Standards page at: `http://drupal.org/node/318`.

After you have entered the contents, save the file to the `formmod` directory. You are done. That's all there is to creating a new module!

Our preceding example uses a single module to hold a single function which contains changes to multiple forms. If you wished instead to implement a single module containing separate functions for each form, you can do so.

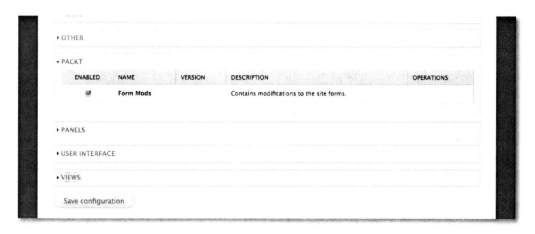

Next, let's activate our new module. Log in to the admin system and head over to the Modules Manager by clicking on **Modules** on the Management menu. Scroll down the list of modules and you will find a new section named **PACKT**, along with our new module, **Form Mods**. You must activate the module and click save to enable this module. Once you have completed this step, the changes made to the forms will be immediately visible.

The Webform Module

If you need a custom form, there is a lot to be said for installing the Webform Module and using it to create and manage your form. Most people will find the option simpler to execute than working with the Form API. Webform allows you to create custom fields of various types and to create complex forms. The module has the added advantage of also providing storage of form results in the site's database and providing a reporting interface for the results gathered by the form.

The module adds a new content type to your site and also allows you to build forms on any content type in the system. This makes it very easy to theme your custom forms. It's fast, it's easy, it simplifies theming, and it has additional advanced features not readily available in the Drupal Form API. For most people, Webforms will be the most attractive solution! See *Chapter 10* to learn more about this module.

Summary

This chapter has covered one of the more challenging areas of Drupal theming, that is, dealing with forms in Drupal. The default forms covered in this chapter can be styled through the application of a variety of techniques, both with and without the assistance of PHPTemplate.

In this chapter, we looked at the various theming techniques and identified the key components associated with each task and where to find them. We also introduced the idea of creating a module to control form modifications, via the function `form_alter`.

In the next chapter, we round up a number of the most common issues users encounter in the course of working with Drupal themes and provide suggestions for dealing with those issues.

9
Overcoming Common Challenges in Drupal Theming

In this chapter we round up an assortment of issues that you are likely to encounter at some point during your Drupal theming efforts. While not all these issues are likely to crop up during any one project, if you work on Drupal themes over time the odds are that you will encounter most of these at some point.

The issues are arranged loosely, from general to more specific. Some of these topics are dealt with in more detail elsewhere, particularly in terms of the principles behind the solutions given. The focus here is on quick fixes to common problems, not on basic skills. Among the topics we cover:

- Cross-browsing compatibility
- Accessibility
- Creating template suggestions for specific features and modules
- Theming Panels
- Theming the Maintenance Page

Let's start with an issue that is common to all themers—how to create themes that work consistently well when viewed in different web browsers.

Maintaining cross-browser compatibility

In an ideal world, you would be able to maintain a consistent appearance for your web pages regardless of the browser used to view them. Unfortunately, it's not an ideal world. The best that can be hoped for is a high degree of consistency, with graceful degradation where that is not possible.

One of the best ways to approach creating a site that works well across platforms is to respect best practices in coding and to strive to write code that is standards compliant. The relevant standards are outlined by the World Wide Web Consortium, commonly known as the **W3C**. In addition to outlining the various standards, their website includes a number of resources. Visit the site at `http://www.w3.org/`.

There are a number of elements involved in creating web pages that comply with standards. Your best bet is to add a validator to your toolkit. Be sure to validate both the CSS and the HTML in your theme. In the next section of this chapter, we discuss several popular validation tools.

 If you look at the source code for Drupal 7, you will see that the system now uses the **doctype definition** (**DTD**) `xhtml-rdfa-1`, but for validation purposes, simply validate against the standard XHTML 1.0 Strict.

While creating consistent and standards compliant code is going to help assure that your site displays well across multiple browsers, it is not going to solve all the problems that can arise. The simple fact is that some browsers — particularly older browsers — lack support for all the current standards and that, while some things will simply be ignored, others might be interpreted in odd ways. The only way to manage this is to test religiously. Maintaining a full browser test bed is difficult, due to the wide number of combinations that exist, but you can certainly download and install the most recent versions of all the popular browsers and use them for your first line testing. For more comprehensive testing, consider one of the services discussed immediately in the following section.

Assessing cross-browser compatibility

The only way to truly assess the effectiveness of your efforts is to test your themes in the various versions of the browsers you are targeting. There are services that provide browser testing on your behalf. The services are often a good option, as they provide access to not only a wider variety of browsers but also to more versions of the same browser. Some services also allow you test how your themes will look on different mobile devices. Among the services to consider are:

Adobe Browser Lab: This convenient and well-designed utility is part of the Adobe CS Live suite of tools. It is available free of charge to owners of Adobe CS5. The tool provides live preview of both static and dynamic web pages. It allows for easy A/B comparisons and basic diagnostics. To use the service, visit `http://browserlab.adobe.com`.

Browsershots: The site provides a free service that allows you to submit a URL, then check back to see screenshots of the page in all the various browsers you select. While free, it can take a while to get results and there is no support for Apple or mobile devices. Visit the site at: `http://www.browsershots.org`.

CrossBrowserTesting: This commercial service offers a very wide range of operating systems and browsers, both traditional and mobile. Want to see how your site looks on Win98 SE running Netscape 4? You can do it here! The service includes both real time testing and a screenshots option. The site is available for a monthly subscription fee, or you can just try it out free for a week. Visit: `http://crossbrowsertesting.com`.

Creating accessible themes

A significant percentage of the web audience has some degree of difficulty reading or navigating websites. As a themer, one of your goals should be to assure that the sites you build are usable by the largest number of people; that means by definition you must account for varying degrees of ability and disability. While creating accessible websites is not only the right thing to do, for many corporate and government websites in America and Europe, it is also a legal issue. Given these imperatives, themers need to have an understanding of the various accessibility standards and what it takes to meet the basic requirements.

The most commonly applied standards for web accessibility are promulgated by the W3C under the name the **Web Accessibility Initiative (WAI)**. A subset of those guidelines, the **Web Content Accessibility Guidelines (WCAG)**, is targeted at web developers. The WAI section of the W3C website includes a large amount of information on what it means to create accessible sites, along with resources to support your efforts.

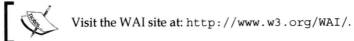

Visit the WAI site at: http://www.w3.org/WAI/.

The first step in creating an accessible site is to establish what level of compliance is required by the site owner. While U.S. corporate and government clients will be concerned about issues like Section 508 compliance, other clients may have different standards. Even within the WCAG there are three levels of compliance—A, AA, and AAA. It's essential that you get a commitment on this issue; the amount of work it takes to meet the various standards is significant and the higher level standards impose considerable limitations on your design discretion.

Section 508 is the standard imposed by the U.S. Government. Learn more: http://www.section508.gov/.

Validation tools

Once you know the standard you must achieve, you will have an outline of the techniques you must implement, and the things you must avoid. Validation tools make it easy for you to identify problem spots and to diagnose issues that relate to compliance with the standards. Having a good validation tool is key to your efforts. There are two excellent plugins for the Firefox browser that provide access to validation tools from directly inside your browser.

The Web Developer add-on for the Firefox browser includes a variety of tools, including your choice of validation tests: CSS, HTML, WAI, and Section 508, among others. The add-on also makes it easy for you to disable JavaScript, change screen color depth, and resize the screen and the fonts—all techniques that make it easier for you to assess how your theme will perform under the various conditions that are likely to exist for at least some of the users in your audience. Download your copy from: https://addons.mozilla.org/en-us/firefox/addon/web-developer/.

A second tool to consider is called Total Validator. To use this tool, you must first download and install the Total Validator application. Once installed, you can also download a Firefox add-on to give you access to the application's features directly from within your browser. It's a (tiny) bit more effort to set up, but well worth it. Total Validator is an excellent validation tool that covers a very wide range of standards. It gives very good feedback, even going so far as to display your source code marked up to show where problems exist. As an added bonus, the application also includes a link checker. To get the Total Validator application, start here: http://www.totalvalidator.com/. Once it is installed, get the Firefox add-on at https://addons.mozilla.org/en-US/firefox/addon/total-validator/.

Drupal theme accessibility basics

Your themes play a key role in Drupal accessibility. Because the themes control the presentation layer, the themes must be designed with accessibility in mind. While the creation of accessible themes is a broad topic, the basic principles covered in this section need to be followed to be successful.

 The Theme Handbook at Drupal.org maintains a good section on improving accessibility at: `http://drupal.org/node/464472`.

Avoiding tables

One of the most fundamental principles of accessibility is to avoid tables. Use CSS for page layout. Tables are not optimal and should be avoided (an exception to this general rule is made only for complex tabular data.) There are a number of good pure CSS themes out there; use one of them as a starting point for your theming efforts if you are not sure where to begin.

Creating accessible forms

Forms are a constant source of frustration for users of all abilities. Adhere to these basic principles and everyone will appreciate you:

- Put your instructions at the top of the form

- Clearly identify required fields; do not rely exclusively on font color!

- Test your field order to make sure users can advance through the form logically using only a keyboard; elements placed out of order cause confusion, and difficulties for many users

- Form field labels need to be closely associated with the fields and should provide additional help where the possibility of ambiguity exists

- Avoid conditional select boxes whose content updates with JavaScript; they will fail where the user has disabled JavaScript

- Make sure that your validation warning messages are clear and unequivocal and do not require users to scroll to view them

- Do not allow your system to dump the user's data in the event of form validation warnings

Not relying on JavaScript

A number of users are working with browsers that do not have JavaScript enabled. If you build a theme that relies on JavaScript for functionality, you need to make sure that the theme degrades gracefully and that alternatives are provided. Always test to make sure the page is navigable with only a keyboard. You also should be aware that JavaScript may cause problems with screen readers.

 This is easy to test—both the Web Developer add-on and Total Validator (discussed previously) let you temporarily disable JavaScript for page testing.

Making sure your text resizes

Use proper CSS coding to assure that the text on the page can be resized by the user's browser. Test this function to assess the impact on your layout.

Ordering elements on the screen logically

Place the page elements in a logical order inside your code. If the visitor views the site without the benefit of the CSS, the logical structure you have created in the code will help maintain the integrity of the page. The use of *skip to* or *jump* links can also help tie things together.

Providing hover states and visited states

Make sure your link classes include both a hover state and a visited state; these indicators make it much easier for users to identify links and to keep track of where they have already been.

Providing alternatives to applets and plugins

If the page requires the use of an applet or plugin, provide a text link to the download of the applet or plugin or provide an alternative for the display of the content.

Supporting a semantic structure

The H tags in HTML are intended to allow the people who create content to impose hierarchical ordering on that content. Proper use of the H tags makes it easy for users to determine the information structure on the page and the relationship between the various parts of the content. When designing your CSS selectors, make sure you provide for the use of H tags in proper sequence and also produce for the content team a style guide to help them apply the styles consistently when they create the page content.

Using system fonts for your menus

Use of image files for your menus is not optimal. In addition to causing accessibility problems they can also slow down page loading and create problems for the search engines. While proper use of the `alt` image attribute can help mitigate this, it is simply better to avoid the whole issue by using text for the menu items.

Using capitalization appropriately

Use of ALL CAPS in your text can cause unintended consequences for screen readers, which may interpret the presence of all caps as an acronym that needs to be spelled out to the listener.

Using a suitable color scheme

Make sure your color selection maintains an appropriate level of contrast for viewers with visual acuity problems. Also remember to test your system in black and white to make sure it remains navigable with the colors turned off.

 Both the Web Developer and Total Validator tools can help you with testing contrast and color depth.

Using jump links

Jump links should be placed at the top of the page to allow visitors to jump directly to the main content or key functionality. This is particularly critical where you have included decorative elements, such as a header image or a piece of Flash, in the space preceding the main page content.

 The Drupal.org site contains a good listing of modules that help with accessibility. Visit: `http://drupal.org/node/394252`.

Creating template suggestions for fields

With the arrival of custom fields in the core of Drupal 7, one of the tricks you need to add to your repertoire is the ability to create template suggestions for custom fields. Drupal makes this easy by giving you a default template to use.

Here's how to set up a template suggestion for a field.

1. Find the machine name of the field you wish to style. Typically this is done by viewing the Content Type which contains the field. Select the **Manage Fields** option next to the name of the content type. On the page that loads you can see a list of all the fields. The **Name** column contains the machine name of the field—that's the data you need.

2. Next, go to the directory /modules/field/theme and copy the file field. tpl.php.

3. Go to your active theme directory, paste in the field.tpl.php file.

4. Rename the file to include the machine name of the field you wish to style. Use this syntax: field--[machinename].tpl.php.

5. Open the file and remove the comment field immediately above the code (The comment begins with this text: **THIS FILE IS NOT TO BE USED...**).

6. Make the changes you desire to the file.

7. Save the file.

8. Clear the theme registry.

You should be able to see your styling on the web page.

You can actually go even further with this technique, and style only the fields that appear on specific content types, by using the following template suggestion structure: field--[machinename]--[type].tpl.php.

Creating template suggestions for specific nodes

PHPTemplate provides a specific template for nodes—node.tpl.php. Using the same principles of precedence we've seen throughout, you can provide template suggestions to suit your needs. To provide a template for the blog node, for example, create node--blog.tpl.php, for the story node, node--story.tpl.php. In the absence of a more specific template, the system will apply the default node.tpl.php file.

The following table shows the suggestions for the default system:

suggestion	affected node
node--blog.tpl.php	blog entries
node--forum.tpl.php	forum entries
node--book.tpl.php	book entries
node--story.tpl.php	story entries
node--page.tpl.php	page entries
node--poll.tpl.php	Polls in node view

Suggestions for key modules

In *Chapter 4, Using Intercepts and Overrides* we discussed at length the process of intercepting and overriding default templates and themable functions. Those templates and functions supply much of the key output on a Drupal site and many are positioned on the page through the assignment of blocks to regions.

In addition to overriding the default template, you can create template suggestions that give you even more granular control over your module output. In this section, we list the template suggestions that are relevant to the key modules in the system.

 Don't forget: If you create a template suggestion, the base template must also be located in the same theme directory!

Styling the Comment module

The comments function in Drupal is controlled by two templates, comment-wrapper.tpl.php and comment.tpl.php. It's worth noting that, in Drupal 7, both of the comment templates are actually displayed inside of the page area that is controlled by the node.tpl.php template. Keep this in mind when you are creating your styling as your comment templates will be impacted by the styling that wraps them inside the node.

The base templates of the comment module can be dynamically styled using the following suggestions:

- The principal comment template, comment.tpl.php, can be styled according to the node type with which the comment is associated by using the syntax comment--[type].tpl.php.

- The default comment wrapper template (`comment-wrapper.tpl.php`) can also be styled according to the node with the syntax `comment-wrapper--[type].tpl.php`.

 Note that the `Comments` module in Drupal also supplies output for the `Forums` module. If you want to style the comments specifically for the forum, use `comment--forum.tpl.php` and `comment-wrapper--forum.tpl.php`.

Styling the Forum module

The base template for the `Forum` module is `forums.tpl.php`. The system also includes two other default templates, `forums-topics.tpl.php` and `forums-containers.tpl.php`. The former handles all forum topics, the latter all forum containers.

There are several options available for creating suggestions that target both forum containers and topics:

Suggestion	Will apply to...
`forums-topics--[forumID].tpl.php`	Forum topics belonging to a forum of a specific ID
`forums-containers--[forumID].tpl.php`	Forum containers belonging to a forum of a specific ID
`forums--[forumID].tpl.php`	Forum of a specific ID

Styling the Poll module

There are multiple default templates for the Poll module.

- `poll-results.tpl.php` handles the poll results for both nodes and blocks. You can target the results in block view by using the suggestion `poll-results--[block].tpl.php`.
- `poll-vote.tpl.php` handles the voting form. You can target the form in block view by using the suggestion `poll-vote--[block].tpl.php`.
- `poll-bar.tpl.php` handles the individual bars in the poll results. You can target the individual bars when displayed in block view by using the suggestion `poll-bar--[block].tpl.php`.

Styling the Profile module

The base template `profile-wrapper.tpl.php` is the template used to display the member listing page for browsing. You can create a suggestion for the template by using the syntax `profile-wrapper--[field].tpl.php`.

Styling the Search module

Drupal provides the `search-results.tpl.php` template for handling the search results; that template can be used as a base template for more specific suggestions.

The search results in the system are automatically categorized as either node or user and the different categories of results are displayed on different tabs on the search results page. To style your search results by type, create one or more of the following:

Suggestion	Will apply to...
`search-results--node.tpl.php`	Controls the node type search results display, as a whole
`search-results--user.tpl.php`	Controls the user type search results display, as a whole
`search-result--node.tpl.php`	Controls individual node type search results
`search-result--user.tpl.php`	Controls individual user type search results

Theming Views

The `Views` module is a powerful tool that enables you to create lists of content items for display on your site. The module is quite popular with Drupal site developers as it provides an easy way to create queries and obtain the output for display as pages or blocks.

As a themer, you are very likely to have to deal with `Views` output at some point in time. Theming views, however, can be a bit tricky if you are unfamiliar with the way the module works. In this section, we take a quick look at the basics of theming `Views`.

 The `Views` module is discussed further in *Chapter 10, Useful Extensions for Themers*.

When **Views** is enabled on a site, you can access the Views **Dashboard** by clicking the **Structure** option on the Management Menu, and then selecting the option **Views**. The Views **Dashboard** shows a list of all the views in the system and provides you with links to edit them, as shown in the following screenshot:

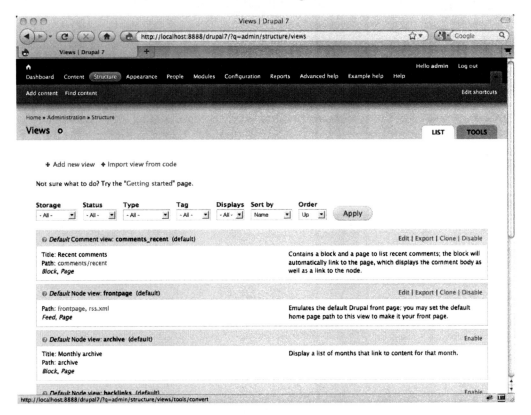

To get to the information you need to begin theming your views, click the **Edit** link next to the view you wish to theme. Clicking the link opens the **Views** editing page. There's a lot of information there, but you are only concerned with a narrow subset of that information.

The first thing you must do is select what it is you wish to theme. If you wish to theme a page view, click the option **Page** at the top left of the screen. If you wish to theme a block view, click the option **Block**. The screen will update, based on your selection. Look for the box labeled **Style settings**—this contains the key information you need.

The **Style settings** box contains information about the layout used by the view. You can update any of the values shown in the box by clicking on them; when you click you will note that the lower portion of the page refreshes, listing the options available for that choice. The most important of the options listed here—at least from a themer's point of view—is the option named **Theme**. Clicking the option **Theme** will present you with a list of all the possible templates and suggestions available for you to theme.

For my example, the front page view. Click **edit**, then select **page**, then click on **Theme: Information** in the **Style settings** box. The following screenshot shows you the **Page Theming information** output, which contains a list of template files.

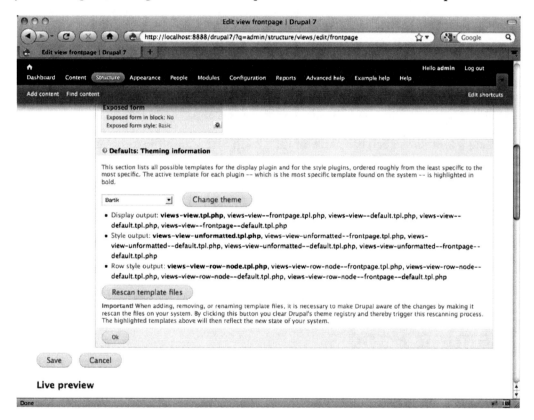

The list of templates is grouped as follows:

* Display output: The templates listed here control the structure of the overall views, including the position of the primary view content.

- Style output: The templates here control the structure of the view's display style, for example, a list, a table, or unformatted output. The templates here will control the view title and the code surrounding each row.

- Row style output: These templates control the internal formatting of the rows.

Additionally, though we do not see it in the preceding example, many views also include a further grouping:

- Fields: The templates listed here will be for each field in the display.

 The Semantic Views module, discussed in *Chapter 10*, provides a useful aid when it comes to theming Fields view styles.

The listing of templates shows you all the possible template files you could use. The list is ordered from the most general to the most specific. Like other templates in the Drupal system, the views template suggestions create a hierarchy, with the more specific templates taking precedence over the more general.

To create a template, click the name of the group containing the template you desire; the page will refresh and show you the code for the base template. Copy the code and create a new file inside the active theme directory. Name it to match the base template or one of the suggestions, as needed. Place your code in the new file, refresh the theme registry, and you are done.

 A basic Views theming tutorial can be found at: `http://drupal.org/node/352970`.

Theming Panels

The Panels module makes it easy for you to create complex layouts without having to create custom templates. With Panels installed on your site, you can build layouts directly from inside the administration system. Each panel can hold any number of elements from your system or even custom content.

 The Panels module is discussed further in *Chapter 10*.

In most cases, the contents of your panels are drawn from existing nodes and modules and the styling of those nodes and modules exhibit will be that supplied by the system for those elements. You will style each of those elements individually, even though the output's positioning on the page is controlled by the panel.

It is possible, however, to embed your own CSS in Panels and thereby effect all the elements contained within the panel. To embed CSS in a panel, select the **Structure** option on the Management Menu. On the page that loads, select **Panels**, then choose the **Edit** link next to the name of the panel you wish to modify. On the **Panel** editing page, click the option **General**. The page reloads, as shown in the following screenshot:

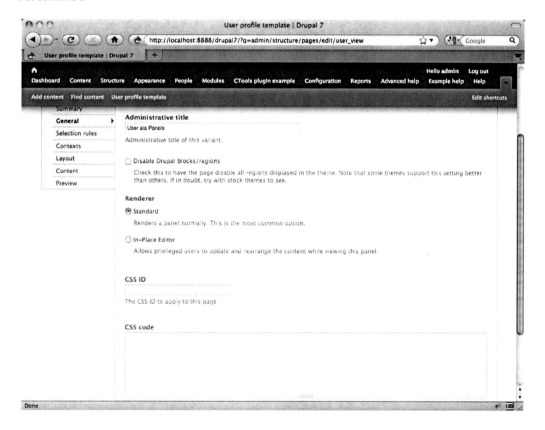

In the **CSS ID** field you can enter the name of the selector you want to apply to the Panel. In the field labeled **CSS-code**, you can even add the full version of the selector if you wish. The better course, however, is to use the theme's stylesheet to hold your **CSS ID**.

If you are adding an existing node to a panel, you also have the option to create a unique identifier for the pane that can then be used to create a template suggestion. To enable this option, edit your panel, then select the **content** option. Click the gear icon for the pane you wish to modify. In the pop up that opens, select **existing node**. The **Configure new Existing node** pop up opens, as shown in the following screenshot:

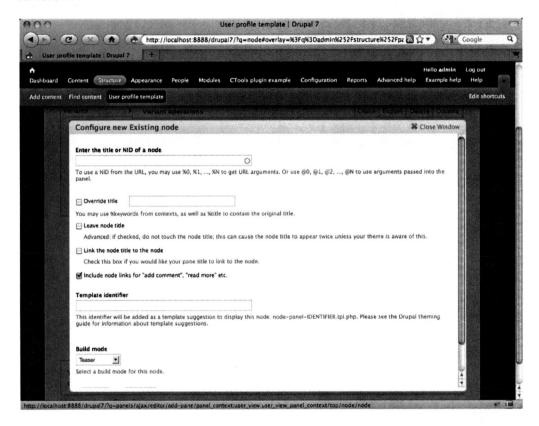

Enter a simple label in the **Template identifier** field. After you save your changes, you can theme this pane by creating a new template by the name of `node-panel-[identifier].tpl.php`.

Theming the maintenance page

If you wish to display a custom template when your site is in maintenance mode, or in the event of a database failure, you can do so by working with the maintenance page functionality. The system includes a default template, located at `/modules/system/maintenance-page.tpl.php`.

To set up your custom maintenance page, there are two steps: First, override the default template file by copying it into your active theme directory. Second, you must also modify your `settings.php` file to instruct the system to display the template. You can do this by enabling the `$conf` variable and adding the internal name of your theme, like this:

```
$conf['maintenance_theme'] = 'themename';
```

Note that your `settings.php` file is likely to be write-protected. You will need to make changes to the permissions to modify the file. Do not forget to change the permissions back after you've finished, in order to protect the file.

If you wish to have a separate template that is used only when there is a database failure, there is a template suggestion available: `maintenance-page--offline.tpl.php`. However, as the database will not be available when that is displayed, you have to hardcode a number of additional items into that template file to get it to display properly. If you wish to explore this topic, please visit `http://drupal.org/node/195435` for a more detailed discussion of what is involved.

Troubleshooting your theme

Face it, it happens: You make a change and something goes thud… Unexpected results sometimes result from mundane actions; when they do, what should you do next?

Writing about troubleshooting is inherently difficult, as it is impossible to anticipate the enormous range of variables that can contribute to any one error. There are, however, some common scenarios that you are likely to encounter at some point. In this section, we try to hit some of those common problems and offer some ideas for solutions.

Basic principles

Before we go into specifics, the following are a few of basic principles you should keep in mind:

Use a validator: As discussed earlier in this chapter, a good validator can help you create standards compliant code and standards compliant code is less likely to create conflicts and inconsistencies.

1. Use sub-themes wherever possible: If something goes horribly wrong, you can always roll things back by reverting to the original base theme files.

2. Test on your development server, not on the live site.

3. Use a theme switcher when upgrading a live theme: If you have to upgrade a theme on a live site, give yourself some room for error by installing a theme switcher module, then assign the new theme to a few private pages to test it before you switch it on for the entire site.

 See *Chapter 10* for some suggested theme switcher modules.

4. Use Firebug to identify styling issues: Highlight the problematic area, right-click, and select **Inspect Element**.

5. When you need a reality check, use Stark. The Stark theme included with the core is intended to help you see only the default system styling. If you can't get to the bottom of a styling issue, switch over to Stark and compare how the problematic element looks with only the default system styling in place.

Troubleshooting common problems

Here are some common problems we've all seen at one time or another:

Problem	Suggestions
I just changed my styling and I can't see any difference.	Make sure you have disabled CSS compression (located in the Performance Manager).
My site is a total wreck in Internet Explorer.	You may have run up against IE's stylesheet limit (31 stylesheets). You can work around this by enabling the Optimize CSS option in the Performance Manager (though enabling this may cause the problem mentioned immediately above!). The only real solution here is to combine some stylesheets to try to get below the limit.
My CSS (or template) overrides are not working.	Clear the cache. Follow that with a hard refresh on your browser.
The dreaded White Screen of Death (that is, I see nothing at all on the screen).	There's a great list of potential causes here: `http://drupal.org/node/158043`.
All my styling has disappeared.	You may have moved or deleted the active theme. If that is not the case, check the path to your CSS by viewing the source of the page.
Neither my styles nor my images are showing up.	Check permissions on the directories that relate to your themes.

Problem	Suggestions
Layout breaks; content overlaps or overflows causing columns to break.	Validate your CSS and check whether you have loaded content that exceeds the maximum space available in one of the columns.
Some of my visitors can't see a page/module/block.	Check the Permissions Manager to make sure all the proper roles have all the necessary privileges.
I can see the home page, but none of the internal pages.	This is likely a problem related somehow to Apache. Likely areas to check are whether `mod_rewrite` is installed and whether your `.htaccess` file is located in the right place.
I can't figure out where the output on the screen comes from.	Install and use the Theme Developer extension.
I can't figure out what template suggestion to use.	Install and use the Theme Developer extension.
My theme's logo/slogan/site name doesn't show up.	Check your theme configuration settings to make sure you have not disabled those functions.
I changed themes and now some of my blocks are gone.	Your new theme probably has different regions than your old theme. When you changed themes, the modules assigned to the missing regions were hidden from view.

If you are having a problem, you are most likely not alone. If you can't sort things out on your own, you might want to consider a visit to the Drupal Support Forum: http://drupal.org/forum.

Summary

This chapter looked at an assortment of issues that you are likely to see during the course of Drupal theming. The list of topics ranges broadly, from the concepts behind building cross-browser compatible sites and working with web accessibility, to troubleshooting common theme problems. In between, we looked at how to use template suggestions to target output in certain narrow circumstances.

The content in this chapter supplements and draws upon the principles discussed in the early chapters of this book and is intended to round up a number of miscellaneous issues that are not conveniently addressed elsewhere in this text.

In the final chapter, we look at extensions and other resources you may find useful during site building and theming.

10

Useful Extensions for Themers

Throughout this book, we have used a variety of tools to demonstrate the various techniques. In addition to a basic toolset made up of an HTML editor, an FTP program, and a browser, we also used several specialized tools. In this chapter, we round up a listing of all the specialized tools used in this book, along with a number of additional items that you may find useful when working on your themes.

Each tool is listed along with a brief synopsis and a URL to the relevant project site. This list should not be viewed as an endorsement of any particular module or product over any other; it is simply my attempt to help you discover some of the tools that are at your disposal.

The tools listed here fall into two categories:

- Drupal modules
- Non-Drupal third-party software

Drupal modules

There exist within the Drupal.org site a number of modules that are relevant to your work of theming a site. Some are straightforward tools that make your standard theming tasks easier, others are extensions to Drupal functionality that enable to you do new things, or to do things from the admin interface that normally would require working with the code. The list here is not meant to be comprehensive, but it does list all the key modules that are either presently available for Drupal 7 or at least in development. There are additional relevant modules that are not listed here, as at the time this was written, they showed no signs of providing a Drupal 7 version.

Caution

One thing to keep in mind here—some of these modules attempt to reduce complex tasks to simple GUI-based admin interfaces. While that is a wonderful and worthy effort, you should be conscious of the fact that sometimes tools of this nature can raise performance and security issues and due to their complexity, sometimes cause conflicts with other modules that also are designed to perform at least part of the functions being fulfilled by the more complex module. As with any new module, test it out locally first and make sure it not only does what you want, but also does not provide any unpleasant surprises.

The modules covered in this chapter include:

- **Administration Menu**
- **Chaos Tool Suit**
- **Colorbox**
- **Conditional Stylesheets**
- **Devel**
- **@font-your-face**
- **Frontpage**
- **HTML5 Tools**
- **.mobi loader**
- **Mobile Theme**
- **Nice Menus**
- **Noggin**
- **Organic Groups**
- **Panels**
- **Semantic Views**
- **Skinr**
- **Style Guide**
- **Sweaver**
- **Taxonomy Theme**
- **Theme Developer**
- **ThemeKey**

- **Views**
- **Webform**

Administration Menu

The Administration Menu was a mainstay of many Drupal sites built during the lifespan of Drupal 6.x. With the arrival of Drupal 7, we thought it unlikely we would need the module, as the new toolbar functionality in the core accomplished a lot of the same thing. In the course of writing this, however, we installed Administration Menu and were pleasantly surprised to find that not only can you run the old-style Administration Menu, but they have also now included the option to run a Toolbar-style Administration Menu, as shown in the following screenshot:

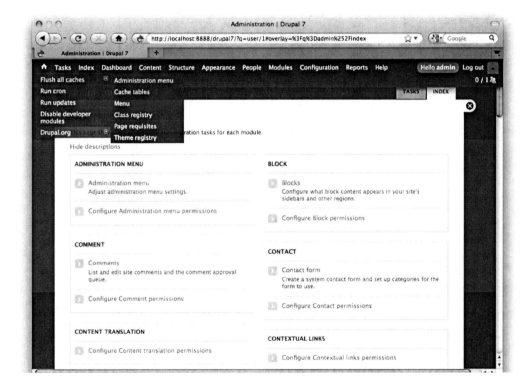

The Administration Menu Toolbar offers all the options of the default Toolbar plus the added advantage of exposing all the menu options without having to navigate through sub-menus on the overlay. Additionally, you have fast access to clearing the caching, running cron, and disabling the Devel module (assuming you have it installed). A great little tweak to the new Drupal 7 administration interface.

View the project at: `http://drupal.org/project/admin_menu`.

Chaos Tool Suite

This module provides a collection of APIs and tools to assist developers. Though the module is required by both the Views and Panels modules, discussed elsewhere in this chapter, it provides other features that also make it attractive. Among the tools to help themers are the Form Wizard, which simplifies the creation of complex forms, and the Dependent widget that allows you to set conditional field visibility on forms. The suite also includes CSS Tools to help cache and sanitize your CSS.

Learn more at `http://drupal.org/project/ctools`.

Colorbox

The Colorbox module for Drupal provides a jQuery-based lightbox plugin. It integrates the third-party plugin of the same name (`http://colorpowered.com/colorbox/`). The module allows you to easily create lightboxes for images, forms, and content. The module supports the most commonly requested features, including slideshows, captions, and the preloading of images.

Colorbox comes with a selection of styles or you can create your own with CSS. To run this module, you must first download and install the Colorbox plugin from the aforementioned URL. Visit the Colorbox Drupal module project page at: `http://drupal.org/project/colorbox`.

Conditional Stylesheets

The module allows themers to easily address cross-browser compatibility issues with Internet Explorer. With this module installed, you can add stylesheets targeting the browser via the theme's `.info` file, rather than having to modify the `template.php` file. The module relies on the conditional comments syntax originated by Microsoft.

To learn more, visit the project site at `http://drupal.org/project/conditional_styles`.

Devel

The Devel module is a suite of tools that are useful to both module and theme developers. The module provides a suite of useful tools and utilities. Among the options it provides:

- Auto-generate content, menus, taxonomies, and users

- Print summaries of DB queries
- Print arrays
- Log performance
- Summaries of node access

The module is also a prerequisite to the Theme Developer module, discussed later in this chapter.

Learn more: `http://drupal.org/project/devel`.

@font-your-face

@font-your-face provides an admin interface for browsing and applying web fonts to your Drupal themes. The module employs the CSS @font-face syntax and draws upon a variety of online font resources, including Google Fonts, Typekit. com, KERNEST, and others. The system automatically loads fonts from the selected sources and you can apply them to the styles you designate—without having to manually edit the stylesheets. It's easy-to-use and has the potential to change the way you select and use fonts on your websites.

@font-your-face requires the Views module to function. Learn more at the project site: `http://drupal.org/project/fontyourface`.

Frontpage

This module serves a very specific purpose—it allows you to designate, from the admin interface, different front pages for anonymous and authenticated users. Though you can accomplish the same thing through use of `$classes` and a bit of work, the module makes it possible for anyone to set this up without having to resort to coding.

Visit the project site at `http://drupal.org/project/frontpage`.

HTML5 Tools

This module, still in development at the time this was written, aims to allow Drupal sites to be built using HTML 5. The module includes multiple tools intended to get HTML5 elements into Drupal, from forms, to DOCTYPE, to markup and the various Drupal entities. This module looks promising, but it is still too early to evaluate it.

Track their progress at `http://drupal.org/project/html5_tools`.

.mobi Loader

The .mobi Loader module is intended to work with the .mobi theme—a specialty theme intended for use specifically on mobile devices. The module automatically detects requesting the .mobi alias of the site and overrides the default theme with the .mobi theme.

View the project at `http://drupal.org/project/mobi_loader`.

Mobile Theme

Mobile Theme is a theme switcher. The module adds the ability for the administrator to designate a theme for use with mobile devices directly from within the Theme Manager. When site visitors access the site on mobile devices, they selected theme will be displayed in preference to the default theme.

Learn more at `http://drupal.org/project/mobile_theme`.

Nice Menus

Need a quick drop-down menu solution? Nice Menus has the answer. This module provides multiple menus with configurable multi-tier menus that can be positioned on your page via the Blocks Manager. The system supports up to ten horizontal and vertical menus with multiple levels. The following screenshot shows a vertical menu configured with a fold right sub-menu:

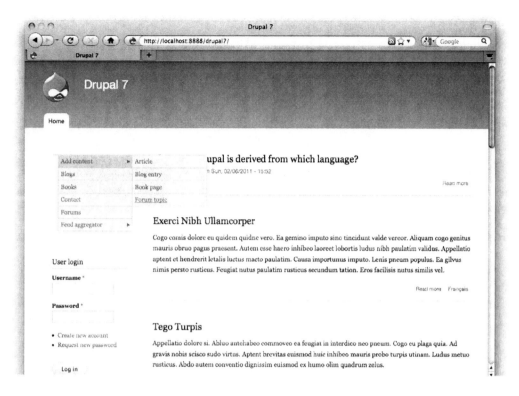

Menus created with Nice Menus are predominantly CSS. You can style them easily by overriding the default selectors. The module developer has also kindly included theme functions that give you even more control over the appearance. The Nice Menus project includes decent documentation to get you started.

Learn more at: `http://drupal.org/project/nice_menus`.

 Two other menu modules to consider are Simple Menu: `http://drupal.org/project/simplemenu` and Mega Menu: `http://drupal.org/project/megamenu`.

Noggin

The Noggin module closes a gap in the core Drupal themes by providing the ability to add a custom header image to the default Drupal themes directly from the Theme Manager. As you can see in the following screenshot, the module adds a new section to the Theme specific configuration settings page:

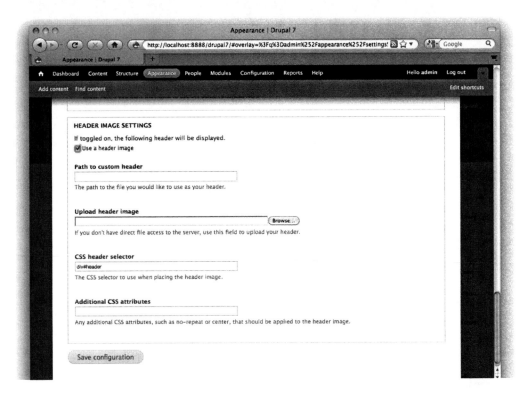

Using the controls on the page, you can upload the header image of your choice to any of the default themes. For themes that employ different markup, you can add a custom CSS selector to enable the functionality.

Visit the project at `http://drupal.org/project/noggin`.

Organic Groups

Organic Groups is not directly about theming, but if you need to enable users to create and manage their own groups, then this module is a lifesaver. We mention it here because the implementation of this module makes it easy to control block and content visibility by group. Additionally, you can also set up the module to provide different themes for different groups of users.

Organic Groups is a very powerful module and quite popular. An entire eco-system of modules has grown up around Organic Groups and there are many options available here. It powers come very big sites and makes building intranet and extranet-type functionality much simpler.

Learn more by visiting the project page: `http://drupal.org/project/og`.

Panels

The Panels module makes the creation of multi-column layouts a breeze. With Panels, you are able to divide a page into content areas and control the content in each area. Blocks and nodes can be mixed freely. The Panels module also allows you to create custom blocks, so-called "mini Panels" using similar logic and tools.

The system comes with several default two and three column formats, but you can do virtually anything you want with a little configuration work. The Panels Everywhere module provides an interesting variation on this functionality, unfortunately, at the time this was written, there was not yet any sign that it would be updated for Drupal 7. Panels require the Chaos Tool Suite module.

Learn more: `http://drupal.org/project/panels`.

Semantic Views

This module extends the Views module functionality. The purpose of the module is to simplify the theming of Views by making it easier to insert HTML markup for your Views rows and fields. Instead of overriding row style templates for views, you can specify the HTML elements and classes from inside the Views UI. You must have the Views module to use this module.

To learn more, visit `http://drupal.org/project/semanticviews`.

Skinr

The Skinr module is drawing a fair amount of attention these days. The module sets out to allow a themer to define a set of reusable CSS styles and to then make those available throughout the Drupal UI. The idea is exciting and holds a tremendous amount of promise for helping rationalize and create manageable CSS structures in the complex world of Drupal stylesheets. Themes do have to be modified slightly to be Skinr compatible, making it more difficult to retrofit Skinr into an existing site (though not impossible by any stretch of the imagination). An increasing number of themes are being made available in Skinr compatible format and as a community begins to grow around the extension we are seeing not only more themes but also more "skins," that is, bundles of reusable style definitions. The module was still under development for Drupal 7 at the time of writing so full evaluation was not possible.

Learn more: `http://drupal.org/project/skinr`.

Style Guide

The Style Guide module does just exactly what the name implies—it produces a visual reference page that lets you check the styling for your theme. Once enabled, a quick visit to the Theme Manager shows a new link next to each theme: Style Guide. Click the link to see a page of sample text showing all the most common page elements and HTML styles compiled in one place, as seen in the following screenshot. A great time-saver and a fast way to check your work, and spot inconsistencies and conflicts in your CSS styling.

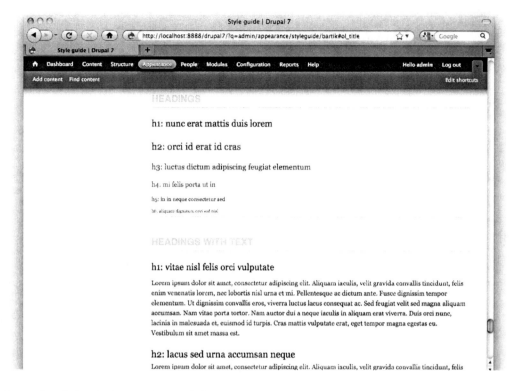

Download the Style Guide module at `http://drupal.org/project/styleguide`.

Sweaver

Sweaver is intended to make themes editable by anyone. With Sweaver installed, the user has an easy-to-use graphical interface inside their browser that allows them to completely change their theme without knowing CSS. You can modify fonts, colors, sizes, and element positions. Once you achieve the look you like, you can save your changes. The following screenshot shows Sweaver in action:

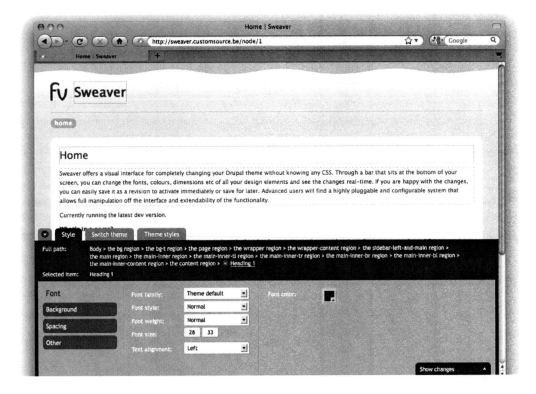

While this module is certainly not for the hardcore themers in the crowd, it does open up Drupal theme customization—at least at the CSS level—to those with little or no coding skills. Sweaver requires Chaos Tool Suite.

Visit the Sweaver project to learn more: `http://drupal.org/project/sweaver`.

Taxonomy Theme

Taxonomy Theme is a simpler and more limited frontend for the ThemeKey functionality, explained next. Taxonomy Theme is focused on providing the ability to change the theme of a given node based on the taxonomy term or vocabulary. Additionally, you can designate themes by path or by views if you are using the Views module. You will need to install ThemeKey to use this module.

Visit the project page at `http://drupal.org/project/taxonomy_theme`.

ThemeKey

The ThemeKey module is an advanced theme switcher that allows you to run multiple themes on your site and to automatically switch between them based on criteria. This not only provides an alternative to relying on multiple page templates and the theme layer, but also perhaps more importantly, lets you designate specific themes to specific types of devices or for older browsers. You can also use it to provide a splash page for your site, or set up promotional landing pages. Moreover, if you have a live site and you want to put a new theme on it, ThemeKey gives you the means to test the new theme on the live site without having to expose the work in progress to visitors.

Download the module from `http://drupal.org/project/themekey`.

Views

The Views module enhances your control over the listing of content items (nodes). With views you can create custom lists that contain the content you want, sorted in the manner you want. Views makes it easy to make blog-site type lists of the most recent articles, most recent comments, top posts in a category, most popular posts, and so on. Essentially a smart query builder, Views is a very powerful module that enables you to really open up your content display in a wide variety of manners. Additionally, it can also be used to generate reports, create summaries, and group and display images.

Views require the Chaos Tool Suite, discussed earlier in this chapter.

Learn more: `http://drupal.org/project/views`.

Webform

The Webform module provides you with enhanced form building capabilities. It enables you to produce complex and advanced forms directly from within the admin interface. Once installed it adds a new content type, which can then be customized to display the fields, controls, and widget you require. The forms support Mollom, CAPTCHA, and form validation.

Once published, submissions of the form are collected inside the system and can also be e-mailed to one or more persons. The data collected in the system can then be displayed and browsed from within the admin interface.

Visit the project page to learn more: `http://drupal.org/project/webform`.

Third-party software

In addition to the wonderful world of Drupal modules, there are third-party software tools that you should consider. Three of the four items on this list are browser plugins. While your preference in browser is entirely your own, all three of the browser plugins are Firefox compatible:

- Drush
- Firebug
- Web Developer Extension
- YSlow

Drush

Drush is a command-line shell and scripting interface for Drupal. The utility can greatly speed your development time — if you are comfortable working with a command-line tool. Though there is a Drush project page on the Drupal.org website, it is not a Drupal module. Drush is a third-party project.

Drush provides tools to execute cron, clear caches, and query the database. Among the many things Drush does well is the rapid installation of modules and themes from the Drupal.org site. You can literally install things with just a few key strokes. If you know what you want, you can grab it and install it in no time at all. Migrating an entire Drupal installation is similarly fast and easy. It's a huge time saver and well worth the effort it takes to get over any dread you may experience at the site of a command line. Visit the Drush home page to learn more at `http://drush.ws`.

The Drush Project page at Drupal.org also has more information: `http://drupal.org/project/drush`.

Firebug

Firebug is a wonderfully useful tool for web developers. As an add-on to the Firefox browser, it stays visible and can be accessed by right-clicking on any object on the screen to allow you to view the code and learn about the styling and attributes. With Firebug you can edit the CSS you see on the screen and monitor and debug the HTML and JavaScript live on the page.

Grab your copy at `https://addons.mozilla.org/en-US/firefox/addon/firebug/`.

Web Developer Extension

The Web Developer Extension is very similar to Firebug but with a few extra tools thrown into the mix, such as the ability to re-size your browser window to preset sizes. Though it seems people use both, many people prefer one over the other.

Grab your copy at `https://addons.mozilla.org/en-US/firefox/`.

YSlow

YSlow is a site performance assessment tool. It is focused on helping you identify how a site performs and where bottlenecks may be. In addition to providing you with a window into how the page loads, it also provides suggestions for improvements. YSlow is a Firefox add-on, but it also integrates with Firebug.

You can get the Firefox YSlow add-on here: `https://addons.mozilla.org/en-us/firefox/addon/yslow`.

Summary

This chapter provides a list of various modules and third-party software tools that can be used to improve your theming experience. The Drupal modules listed cover a wide variety of functionality, from simple utilities to complex GUI-driven theming interfaces. Additional modules like Views and Panels cross over from theming into site building and provide you with fantastic tools for controlling the organization and presentation of output on the page. The third-party software tools are dominated by a list of add-ons for the Firefox browser, but also include the powerful Drush command-line shell and scripting interface for Drupal.

There are plenty of other modules out there and as this was written in the early days of Drupal 7, there will certainly be more appearing. Consider this list a starting point for your explorations.

Identifying Templates, Stylesheets, and Themable Functions

The output of the Drupal system is subject to formatting via three primary elements: templates, stylesheets, and themable functions. These various elements are scattered throughout the Drupal distribution and may not, at first glance, be obvious. Accordingly, one of the most important keys to the success of your theming efforts is the ability to identify and locate the elements that impact the presentation layer. In this chapter, we'll take you on a guided tour of all the system's various templates, stylesheets, and themable functions, as a precursor to learning how to intercept and override these elements in later chapters.

[If a module is not listed here, there are no distinct themable elements associated with the module.]

A guide to Theming Elements

With the large assortment of templates, stylesheets, and themable functions available to you in the default Drupal distribution, finding exactly what you need can sometimes be a bit of a challenge. In an effort to simplify the process of isolating relevant theming elements, we present in the pages that follow a list of the elements organized relative to the functionality they affect.

Common Theme System functions

The `theme.inc` file controls the Drupal theme system. In addition to initializing and loading the theme system, the file contains a number of themable functions that relate specifically to various key elements in Drupal. The functions can be found in two files: `includes/theme.inc` and `includes/theme.maintenance.inc`.

Here is a table of the themable functions and a description of each one:

Function	Path	Description
theme_breadcrumb	includes/theme.inc	Handles the breadcrumb trail.
theme_disable	includes/theme.inc	Disables a list of themes.
theme_enable	includes/theme.inc	Enables a list of themes.
theme_feed_icon	includes/theme.inc	Enables a feed icon.
theme_get_registry	includes/theme.inc	Gets the theme registry.
theme_get_setting	includes/theme.inc	Retrieves a setting for a theme.
theme_get_suggestions	includes/theme.inc	Generates an array of suggestions from path arguments.
theme_html_tag	includes/theme.inc	Returns HTML for a tag with attributes.
theme_image	includes/theme.inc	Themes an image.
theme_indentation	includes/theme.inc	Provides a div for standardizing indentation.
theme_item_list	includes/theme.inc	Returns a themed list of items.
theme_link	includes/theme.inc	Returns HTML for a link.
theme_links	includes/theme.inc	Returns HTML for a list of links.
theme_mark	includes/theme.inc	Returns a themed marker for content (for example, new, updated).
theme_more_help_link	includes/theme.inc	Produces the more help link.
theme_more_link	includes/theme.inc	Produces the more link seen in blocks.
theme_progress_bar	includes/theme.inc	Displays the percentage complete progress bar.
theme_render_template	includes/theme.inc	Renders a system default template.
theme_status_messages	includes/theme.inc	Formats status and error messages.
theme_table	includes/theme.inc	Formats a table.

Function	Path	Description
theme_tablesort_indicator	includes/theme.inc	Produces the sort icon.
theme_username	includes/theme.inc	Formats the username.

Theming the Aggregator module

The Aggregator module provides a variety of functions related to the aggregation and display of syndicated content feeds (for example, RSS, RDF, and Atom).

Default templates

Theming the Aggregator module is made easier in Drupal 7 through the addition of several dedicated template files:

- aggregator-feed-source.tpl.php
- aggregator-item.tpl.php
- aggregator-summary-item.tpl.php
- aggregator-summary-items.tpl.php
- aggregator-wrapper.tpl.php

The default templates are located at modules/aggregator/.

aggregator-feed-source.tpl.php

Provides a template for formatting the source of a feed. When a user is browsing the feed, they will see the output above the feed listings. The available variables include:

Variable	Description
$last_checked	When the feed was last checked (locally).
$source_description	The description text – from the source of the feed.
$source_icon	This is the feed's icon – from the source of the feed.
$source_image	The image associated with the feed – from the source of the feed.
$source_url	The URL to the source of the feed.

aggregator-item.tpl.php

Formats an individual feed item. The available variables include:

Variable	Description
$categories	Categories assigned to the feed.
$content	The content of the individual feed item.
$feed_title	The title of the feed item – from the source of the feed.
$feed_url	The URL of the feed item – from the source of the feed.
$source_date	The date of the item – from the source of the feed.
$source_title	The title of the provider of the feed – from the source of the feed.
$source_url	The URL to the source of the feed.

aggregator-summary-item.tpl.php

Themes a linked feed item for summaries. The available variables include:

Variable	Description
$feed_age	The age of the remote feed.
$feed_title	The title of the feed item – from the source of the feed.
$feed_url	The URL of the feed item – from the source of the feed.
$source_title	The title of the provider of the feed – from the source of the feed.
$source_url	The URL to the source of the feed.

aggregator-summary-items.tpl.php

Themes a presentation of feeds as list items. The available variables include:

Variable	Description
$summary_list	The unordered list of feed items.
$source_url	The URL to the local source (or category).
$title	The title of the feed (or category).

aggregator-wrapper.tpl.php

Wraps aggregator content. The available variables include:

Variable	Description
$content	The entire aggregator contents.
$page	Pagination links.

Default stylesheets

Two stylesheets are dedicated to the formatting of the comments. Both are located at `/modules/aggregator`.

File	Description
`aggregator.css`	Affects the RSS/Newsfeed Aggregator Module and its contents.
`aggregator-rtl.css`	A stylesheet that is used when the site employs right-to-left text orientation.

Themable functions

There are a number of themable functions that relate to the aggregator. The functions can be found in two files: `modules/aggregator/aggregator.module` and `modules/aggregator/aggregator.pages.inc`.

Function	Path	Description
`theme_aggregator_block_item`	`modules/aggregator/aggregator.module`	Formats an individual feed item displayed in a block.
`theme_aggregator_catagorize_items`	`modules/aggregator/aggregator.pages.inc`	Returns HTML for the aggregator page list form for assigning categories.
`theme_aggregator_page_opml`	`modules/aggregator/aggregator.pages.inc`	Allows you to theme the output of the OPML feed.
`theme_aggregator_page_rss`	`modules/aggregator/aggregator.pages.inc`	Allows you to theme the output of the RSS feed.

Theming the Block module

The Block module provides the mechanism for managing the blocks on the page.

Default templates

The system includes only two template files dedicated to blocks:

- `block.tpl.php`
- `block-admin-display-form.tpl.php`

The `block.tpl.php` template can be found at `modules/system/`.

The `block-admin-display-form.tpl.php` template can be found at `modules/block/`.

block.tpl.php

This is the key template for formatting blocks. The available variables include:

Variable	Description
$block->delta	The numeric ID associated with the module.
$block_html_id	A valid HTML ID.
$block->module	The module that generated the block.
$block->region	The region that contains the block.
$block->subject	The block title.
$block_id	ID unique to the block in the region.
$block_zebra	Provides an "odd/even" marker for the block. Alternates for each block used within a region.
$classes	String of classes that can be used to add contextual CSS styling.
$classes_array	An array of HTML class attributes. This is a helper variable and is flattened into a string within the variable $classes.
$content	The block content.
$id	Similar to $block_id but not dependent upon the region.
$is_admin	Returns True if user is an administrator.
$is_front	Returns True if user is viewing the front page.
$logged_in	Returns True if user is logged in and authenticated.
$title_prefix	An array of additional output intended to be displayed in front of the main title tag.
$title_suffix	An array of additional output intended to be displayed after the main title tag.
$zebra	Provides an "odd/even" marker for block but is not region dependent.

block-admin-display-form.tpl.php

The template controls the admin system's block configuration interface. The available variables include:

Variable	Description
$block_listing	An array of blocks keyed to region and delta.
$block_regions	The title of the region of the block.
$form_submit	The submit form button.

Default stylesheets

There is one style sheet dedicated to the block module. It is located at: `/modules/block`.

File	Description
`block.css`	Provides basic selectors for the styling of the block management admin interface

Theming the Book functionality

The Book module creates a node that allows for the creation of hierarchically organized groups of content items, united by a table of contents and common pagination. The book module provides the functions that impact book content and output.

Default templates

The default system includes four default template files dedicated to the book functionality:

- `book-all-books-block.tpl.php`
- `book-export-html.tpl.php`
- `book-navigation.tpl.php`
- `book-node-export-html.tpl.php`

The templates can be found at `modules/book/`.

book-all-books-block.tpl.php

The template renders book outlines within a block. The available variables include:

Variable	Description
`$book_menus`	An array of the book outline. Presented as an unordered list.

book-export-html.tpl.php

This template handles the printed version of the book outline. The available variables include:

Variable	Description
$base_url	The URL to the home page.
$contents	The nodes within the book outline.
$head	The header tags.
$language	The code indicating the language used.
$language_rtl	Returns True when the site uses right-to-left text orientation.
$title	The node's title.

book-navigation.tpl.php

Provides a template for formatting the navigation associated with a book node. The available variables include:

Variable	Description
$book_id	The ID of the current book being viewed.
$book_title	The title of the current book being viewed.
$book_url	The URL of the current book being viewed.
$current_depth	The current node's depth inside the outline.
$has_links	Returns True whenever the parent, previous, or next function has a value.
$next_title	The title of the next node.
$next_url	The URL of the next node.
$parent_title	The title of the parent node.
$parent_url	The URL of the parent node.
$prev_title	The title of the previous node.
$prev_url	The URL of the previous node.
$tree	The children of the current node, rendered as an unordered list.

book-node-export-html.tpl.php

Provides a template for formatting a printer-friendly version of the node. The available variables include:

Variable	Description
$children	All the child nodes associated.

Variable	Description
`$content`	The content of the node.
`$depth`	The current node's depth inside the outline.
`$title`	The title of the node.

Default stylesheets

Two stylesheets are dedicated to the formatting of books. Both are located at `/modules/book`.

File	Description
`book.css`	Controls the formatting of Book node content.
`book-rtl.css`	A stylesheet that is used when the site employs right-to-left text orientation.

Themable functions

There are only two themable functions that relate to books. The functions can be found in two locations: `modules/book/book.module` and `modules/book/book.admin.inc`.

Function	Path	Description
`theme_book_admin_table`	`modules/book/book.admin.inc`	Themes the book administration page.
`theme_book_title_link`	`modules/book/book.module`	Provides the HTML output for the link to the book title, when it is used as a block title.

Theming the Color module

The Color module provides the color change functionality seen in the theme configuration manager of some themes.

Default templates

There are no default templates provided for the Color module.

Default stylesheets

Two stylesheets are dedicated to the Color module. Both are located at /modules/color.

File	Description
color.css	Controls the Color module used with some themes.
color-rtl.css	A stylesheet that is used when the site employs right-to-left text orientation.

Themable functions

There is only one themable function associated with the Color module:

Function	Path	Description
theme_color_scheme_form	modules/color/color.module	Controls formatting of the Color Module form.

Theming the Comment functionality

The comment functionality allows users to add comments to published content.

Default templates

Theming the comments is Drupal 7 is handled by two dedicated template files:

- comment-wrapper.tpl.php
- comment.tpl.php

The default templates are located at modules/comment/.

comment-wrapper.tpl.php

This template is used to wrap all the comments. It is a container that controls the overall formatting of the comment area. The available variables include:

Variable	Description
$classes	String of classes that can be used to provide contextual CSS styling.
$classes-array	Array of HTML class attributes, flattened into a string within the variable $classes.
$content	Handles all the comments for a particular page.

Variable	Description
$node	The node object the comments are attached to.
$title_prefix	An array of additional output that is displayed in front of the main title tag.
$title_suffix	An array of additional output that is displayed after the main title tag.

comment.tpl.php

This is the primary template for controlling the appearance of a comment. The available variables include:

Variable	Description
$author	The name of the author of the comment.
$changed	Date and time comment was last changed.
$classes	String of classes that can be used to provide contextual CSS styling.
$comment	The full comment object.
$content	The main body of the comment.
$created	Date and time comment was created.
$date	The date and time the comment was posted.
$links	The links associated with the functionality.
$new	A marker that indicates a new comment.
$node	The node object the comments are attached to.
$permalink	Comment's permalink.
$picture	The author's picture.
$signature	The author's signature.
$status	The status of the comment (that is, published, unpublished, and so on).
$submitted	**Submitted by** text with date and time.
$title	The title of the comment, linked to the comment body.
$title_prefix	An array of additional output that is displayed in front of the main title tag.
$title_suffix	An array of additional output that is displayed after the main title tag.

Default stylesheets

Two stylesheets are dedicated to the formatting of the comments. Both are located at `/modules/comment`.

File	Description
`comment.css`	This is a very limited stylesheet which essentially only provides the indent style for comments.
`comment-rtl.css`	A stylesheet that is used when the site employs right-to-left text orientation.

Themable functions

There are only two themable functions that relate to the comment functionality. The functions can be found at: `modules/comment/comment.module`.

Function	Path	Description
`theme_comment_block`	`modules/comment/comment.module`	Formats the list of recent comments displayed within a block.
`theme_comment_post_forbidden`	`modules/comment/comment.module`	Controls the **you can't post comments** function.

Theming the Dashboard module

The Dashboard module handles the administration interface dashboard. As there is no frontend output from this module, the theming options are limited.

Default templates

There are no default templates provided for the dashboard functionality.

Default stylesheets

There is one stylesheet dedicated to the formatting of the dashboard. It is located at `/modules/dashboard`.

File	Description
`dashboard.css`	This stylesheet provides the styling of the dashboard.

Themable functions

There are several themable functions associated with the Dashboard module. The functions can be found at: `modules/filter/dashboard.module`.

Function	Path	Description
theme_dashboard	modules/dashboard/dashboard.module	Returns the HTML for the entire dashboard
theme_dashboard_admin	modules/dashboard/dashboard.module	The HTML for the non-customizable portion of the dashboard.
theme_dashboard_region	modules/dashboard/dashboard.module	Styling for the generic dashboard region.
theme_dashboard_disabled_blocks	modules/dashboard/dashboard.module	Styling for a set of disabled blocks.
theme_dashboard_disabled_block	modules/dashboard/dashboard.module	Styling for a disabled block.

Theming the DBLog module

The DBLog records system events and allows administrators to monitor their system. There is no frontend functionality associated with this module, hence the theming options are limited.

Default templates

There are no default templates provided for the DBLog module.

Default stylesheets

Two stylesheets are dedicated to the formatting of the dblog. Both are located at `/modules/dblog`.

File	Description
dblog.css	Provides the styles for the dblog admin interface.
dblog-rtl.css	A stylesheet that is used when the site employs right-to-left text orientation.

Themable functions

There is only one themable function associated with the DBLog module.

Function	Path	Description
`theme_dblog_message`	`modules/dblog/dblog.admin.inc`	Returns the HTML for a log message.

Theming the Field module

The Field module powers the custom field creation.

Default templates

There is one dedicated template file:

•   * field.tpl.php

The default template is located at `modules/field/theme`.

field.tpl.php

This template is not actually used in the system, but is simply provided as a starting point for customization. If needed, copy and place in the active theme directory. The available variables include:

Variable	Description
`$classes`	String of classes that can be used to provide contextual CSS styling.
`$classes-array`	Array of HTML class attributes, flattened into a string within the variable `$classes`.
`$element['#field_language']`	The field language.
`$element['#field_name']`	The field name.
`$element['#field_translatable']`	Whether the field is translatable.
`$element['#field_type']`	The field type.
`$element['#label_display']`	The position of the label display.

Variable	Description
`$element['#view_mode']`	View mode – full or teaser.
`$field_name_css`	CSS compatible field name.
`$field_type_css`	CSS compatible field type.
`$items`	An array of field values.
`$label`	The item label.
`$label_hidden`	Whether the label is set to hidden.

Default stylesheets

Two stylesheets are dedicated to the formatting of the field. Both are located at `/modules/field/theme`.

File	Description
`field.css`	A limited set of styles for the fields and the field form.
`field-rtl.css`	A stylesheet that is used when the site employs right-to-left text orientation.

Themable functions

There are several themable functions associated with the Field module. The functions can be found in three files: `modules/field/field.module`, `modules/field/field.form.inc`, and `modules/field/modules/options/options.module`.

Function	Path	Description
`theme_field`	`modules/field/field.module`	The HTML for a field.
`theme_field_multiple_value_form`	`modules/field/field.form.inc`	HTML for an individual form element.
`theme_options_none`	`modules/field/modules/options/options.module`	The HTML for the label for values not required.

Theming the Field UI module

The Field UI module gives an interface for managing custom fields. As there is no frontend output from this module, the theming options are limited.

Default templates

There are no dedicated templates file.

Default stylesheets

Two stylesheets are dedicated to the formatting of the field. Both are located at /modules/field_ui.

File	Description
field_ui.css	Basic styling for the fields user interface.
field_ui-rtl.css	A stylesheet that is used when the site employs right-to-left text orientation.

Themable functions

There is one themable function associated with the Field UI module. The function can be found at: modules/field_ui/field_ui.admin.inc.

Function	Path	Description
theme_field_ui_table	modules/field_ui/field_ui.admin.inc	The HTML for Field UI overview tables.

Theming the File module

The File module provides the file field.

Default templates

There are no dedicated template files.

Default stylesheets

There is one stylesheet for the File module, located at /modules/file.

File	Description
file.css	Basic styling for the file element.

Themable functions

There are several themable functions associated with the File module. The functions can be found at: `modules/file/file.field.inc`.

Function	Path	Description
`theme_file_formatter_table`	`modules/file/file.field.inc`	Styling for the file attachments table.
`theme_file_icon`	`modules/file/file.field.inc`	HTML for the icon associated with the file type.
`theme_file_link`	`modules/file/file.field.inc`	HTML for a link to the file.
`theme_file_managed_file`	`modules/file/file.field.inc`	Styling for a managed file element.
`theme_file_upload_help`	`modules/file/file.field.inc`	Styling for the help text for the file uploader.
`theme_file_widget`	`modules/file/file.field.inc`	HTML for an individual file upload widget.
`theme_file_widget_multiple`	`modules/file/file.field.inc`	HTML for a group of file upload widgets.

Theming the Filter module

The Filter module allows administrators to specify the text input formats for the site and filter out things that are potentially malicious or harmful. As there is no frontend output from this module, the theming options are limited.

Default templates

There are no default templates provided for the filter functionality.

Default stylesheets

There is one stylesheet for the Filter module, located at `/modules/filter`.

File	Description
`filter.css`	Basic styling for the filter functionality.

Themable functions

There are several themable functions associated with the Filter module. The functions can be found in three files: `modules/filter/filter.module`, `modules/filter/filter.admin.inc`, and `modules/filter/filter.pages.inc`.

Function	Path	Description
theme_filter_admin_ format_filter_order	modules/filter/filter. admin.inc	HTML for a text format's filter order form.
theme_filter_admin_ overview	modules/filter/filter. admin.inc	Themes the admin overview form for filters.
theme_filter_ guidelines	modules/filter/filter. admin.inc	HTML for guidelines for a text format.
theme_filter_tips	modules/filter/filter. pages.inc	Formats the filter tips.
theme_filter_tips_ more_info	modules/filter/filter. module	Formats the filter tips **more info** link.
theme_text_format_ wrapper	modules/filter/filter. module	HTML for a text format enabled form element.

Theming the Form functionality

Handles the various forms and their elements.

Default templates

There are no default templates provided for the form functionality.

Default stylesheets

There are no stylesheets dedicated to the form functionality.

Themable functions

There exists a large number of themable functions associated with forms. The functions can be found at: `includes/form.inc`.

Function	Path	Description
theme_button	includes/form.inc	Formats a button.
theme_checkbox	includes/form.inc	Formats an individual checkbox.
theme_checkboxes	includes/form.inc	Handles a set of checkboxes.

Function	Path	Description
theme_container	includes/form.inc	The HTML to wrap the child elements in a container.
theme_date	includes/form.inc	Formats the date selection element.
theme_fieldset	includes/form.inc	Formats a group of form items.
theme_file	includes/form.inc	Formats a file upload field.
theme_form	includes/form.inc	Provides an anonymous <div> for forms to help satisfy XHTML compliance requirements.
theme_form_element	includes/form.inc	Returns a themed form element, including the **this field is required** message.
theme_form_element_label	includes/form.inc	HTML for a form element label.
theme_form_required_marker	includes/form.inc	The HTML for the "required" marker.
theme_hidden	includes/form.inc	Formats a hidden form field.
theme_image_button	includes/form.inc	Handles formatting of a form image button.
theme_menu_link	includes/form.inc	Styling for a menu link and submenu.
theme_menu_local_action	includes/form.inc	Formats a single local action link.
theme_menu_local_task	includes/form.inc	Formats a single local task link.
theme_menu_local_tasks	includes/form.inc	Formats the primary and secondary local tasks.
theme_menu_tree	includes/form.inc	The HTML for a wrapper for a menu sub-tree.
theme_password	includes/form.inc	Formats a password field.
theme_radio	includes/form.inc	Formats a radio button.
theme_radios	includes/form.inc	Formats a set of radio buttons.
theme_select	includes/form.inc	Formats a drop-down menu or scrolling selection box.
theme_submit	includes/form.inc	Formatting of the submit button on a form.

Function	Path	Description
theme_tableselect	includes/form.inc	HTML for a table with select controls (that is, radio buttons or checkboxes).
theme_textarea	includes/form.inc	Formats a text area within a form.
theme_textfield	includes/form.inc	Formats a text field within a form.
theme_vertical_tabs	includes/form.inc	Formats an element's children as vertical tabs

 Forms are discussed in greater length in *Chapter 8, Dealing with Forms.*

Theming the Forum module

The Forum module handles the threaded discussion forums in Drupal. As this is a fairly complex module with a significant role on the frontend of the system, it is not surprising that there are a number of options available for theming this functionality.

Default templates

The default system includes five default template files dedicated to the forum functionality:

- forum-icon.tpl.php
- forum-list.tpl.php
- forum-submitted.tpl.php
- forum-topic-list.tpl.php
- forums.tpl.php

The templates can be found at modules/forum/.

forum-icon.tpl.php

Displays the icon associated with a post (for example, new, sticky, closed, and so on). The available variables include:

Variable	Description
$first_new	Indicator showing that the item is the first topic with new posts.
$icon	The icon to be displayed.
$new_posts	Indicates whether the topic includes any new posts.

forum-list.tpl.php

Template to control the display of the list of forums and containers. The available variables include:

Variable	Description
$forum_id	The ID of the current forum.
$forum->depth	Depth of forum within content hierarchy.
$forum->description	Forum's description
$forum->is_container	TRUE if the forum containers other forums.
$forum->last_reply	Last time a forum was posted or commented on.
$forum->link	URL of the forum.
$forum->name	Forum's name.
$forum->new_topics	TRUE if the forum contains unread posts.
$forum->new_text	Tells how many new posts.
$forum->new_url	URL to unread posts.
$forum->num_posts	Total number of posts in forum.
$forum->old_topics	Count of posts already read.
$forum->zebra	Even or odd string used for row classes.
$forums	An array of forums and containers.

forum-submitted.tpl.php

This template controls the **submitted by...** information. The available variables include:

Variable	Description
$author	The name of the author of the post.
$time	When the post was made.
$topic	The raw post data.

forum-topic-list.tpl.php

This template displays a list of the forum topics. The available variables include:

Variable	Description
$header	The table header.
$pager	The pagination elements.
$topic_id	Numerical ID for current topic.
$topics	An array of the topics.
$topic->comment_count	The number of replies to the topic.
$topic->created	When the topic was posted.
$topic->icon	The icon.
$topic->last_reply	When the topic was last replied to.
$topic->message	The explanation and link for when a topic has been moved.
$topic->moved	Flag to indicate a moved topic.
$topic->new_replies	Flag to indicate unread comments.
$topic->new_text	Text containing the count.
$topic->new_url	URL to any unread replies.
$topic->timestamp	Raw timestamp for when topic was posted.
$topic->title	The title of the topic.
$topic->zebra	Even or odd string used for row classes.

forums.tpl.php

The template for the forum as a whole. The available variables include:

Variable	Description
$forums	The forums to be displayed.
$forums_defined	A flag to indicate whether the forum has been defined.
$topics	The topics to be displayed.

Default stylesheets

Two stylesheets are dedicated to the formatting of the forums. Both are located at `/modules/forum`.

File	Description
forum.css	Affects the contents of the forum module.
forum-rtl.css	A stylesheet that is used when the site employs right-to-left text orientation.

Themable functions

There is one additional themable function associated with the forum module:

Function	Path	Description
theme_forum_form	modules/forum/forum.admin.inc	Formats the Forum form.

Theming the Help module

The Help module powers the context-sensitive help information, most often seen in the admin interface.

Default templates

There are not default templates dedicated to the help functionality.

Default stylesheets

There are two stylesheets dedicated to the Help module. Both are located at `/modules/help`.

File	Description
help.css	Contains two selectors to style the help function.
help-rtl.css	A stylesheet that is used when the site employs right-to-left text orientation.

Themable functions

There are no additional themable functions associated with the help messages.

Theming the Image functionality

The Image module assists with the image field and image management.

Default templates

There are no default templates dedicated to the image functionality.

Default stylesheets

There are three stylesheets dedicated to the image module. They are located at `/modules/image`.

File	Description
`image.css`	Provides selectors for preview and the widget.
`image-rtl.css`	A stylesheet that is used when the site employs right-to-left text orientation.
`image.admin.css`	Selectors for the admin view.

Themable functions

There are multiple themable functions related to the image functionality. They can be found in three separate files:

Function	Path	Description
`theme_image_anchor`	`modules/image/admin.inc`	Formats the 3x3 grid of checkboxes for image anchors.
`theme_image_crop_summary`	`modules/image/admin.inc`	HTML for summary of image crop effect.
`theme_image_formatter`	`modules/image/field.inc`	HTML for the image field formatter.
`theme_image_resize_summary`	`modules/image/admin.inc`	HTML for summary of image resize effect.
`theme_image_rotate_summary`	`modules/image/admin.inc`	HTML for summary of image rotate effect.
`theme_image_scale_summary`	`modules/image/admin.inc`	HTML for summary of image scale effect.
`theme_image_style`	`modules/image/image.module`	Formats an image using a specific style.
`theme_image_style_effects`	`modules/image/admin.inc`	HTML for the listing of the effects in a specific image style.

Function	Path	Description
theme_image_style_list	modules/image/admin.inc	Formats the page containing the list of image styles.
theme_image_style_preview	modules/image/admin.inc	HTML for the preview of an image style.
theme_image_widget	modules/image/field.inc	Formats the image field widget.

Theming the Locale functionality

The Locale module enables administrators to manage a site's interface languages.

Default templates

There are no default templates dedicated to the locale functionality.

Default stylesheets

There is only one stylesheet dedicated to the Locale module. It is located at /modules/locale.

File	Description
locale.css	Provides a selector for the Locale module.

Themable functions

There are three themable functions related to the locale functionality:

Function	Path	Description
theme_locale_date_format_form	includes/locale.admin.inc	Formats the local date format form.
theme_locale_languages_configure_form	includes/locale.admin.inc	HTML for a language configuration page.
theme_locale_languages_overview_form	includes/locale.admin.inc	Themes the locale admin manager form.

Theming the Menu functionality

The Menu module allows administrators to customize the site navigation menu.

Default templates

There are no default templates dedicated to the Menu module.

Default stylesheets

There is only one stylesheet dedicated to the Menu module. It is located at `/modules/menu`.

File	Description
`menu.css`	Provides three selectors for the menu module.

Themable functions

There are only two themable functions that relate to the Menu module.

Function	Path	Description
`theme_menu_admin_overview`	`module/menu/menu.admin.inc`	HTML for the menu title and description for the menu overview page.
`theme_menu_overview_form`	`module/menu/menu.admin.inc`	Themes the menu overview form.

Theming the Node functionality

The Node module allows content to be submitted to the site, in various forms.

Default templates

The Node module provides a single dedicated template file, but it is key. This one template provides many formatting options and handles all node content:

* `modules/node/node.tpl.php`

node.tpl.php

This template controls node display. This is a powerful and important template and accordingly there are a number of variables associated with it:

Variable	Description
`$classes`	String of classes that can be used to provide contextual CSS styling.
`$classes-array`	Array of HTML class attributes; flattened into a string within the variable `$classes`.

Variable	Description
`$comment`	The comment settings for the node.
`$comment_count`	The number of comments tied to the node.
`$content`	The node body and/or teaser.
`$created`	The time the node was published.
`$date`	The creation date of the node.
`$display_submitted`	Whether submission information should be displayed.
`$id`	The position of the node.
`$is_admin`	Returns True when the current user is an administrator.
`$is_front`	Returns True when the current page is the front page.
`$logged_in`	Returns True when the current user is logged in and authenticated.
`$name`	The username of the node's author.
`$node`	The full node object.
`$node_url`	The URL of the current node.
`$page`	Flag indicating full page state.
`$promote`	Flag indicating from page promotion state.
`$readmore`	Flag indicating length of node exceeds teaser limit.
`$status`	Flag indicating published state.
`$sticky`	Flag indicating sticky state.
`$submitted`	The **submitted by...** information.
`$teaser`	Flag indicating the teaser state.
`$title`	The node's title.
`$title_prefix`	An array of additional output that is displayed before the main title tag.
`$title_suffix`	An array of additional output that is displayed after the main title tag.
`$type`	The node type (for example, story, blog, and so on).
`$uid`	The user ID of the node's author.
`$user_picture`	The picture of the node's author.
`$view_mode`	The view of the node (that is, teaser, full).
`$zebra`	Even or odd string used for row classes.

Default stylesheets

Two stylesheets are dedicated to the node module. Both are located at: `/modules/node`.

File	Description
`node.css`	Provides selectors for nodes.
`node-rtl.css`	A stylesheet that is used when the site employs right-to-left text orientation.

Themable functions

There are a number of themable functions that relate to the node functionality. The functions can be found in three files: `modules/node/node.module`, `modules/node/node.admin.inc`, and `modules/node/node.pages.inc`.

Function	Path	Description
`theme_node_add_list`	`modules/node/node.pages.inc`	Displays the list of available node types.
`theme_node_admin_overview`	`modules/node/content_types.inc`	Formats the node administration overview.
`theme_node_preview`	`modules/node/node.pages.inc`	The node preview used during content creation and editing.
`theme_node_recent_block`	`modules/node/node.module`	Formats a list of recent content.
`theme_node_recent_content`	`modules/node/node.module`	Formats the recent node displayed in the recent content block.
`theme_node_search_admin`	`modules/node/node.module`	Renders the admin node search form.

Theming the OpenID module

The OpenID module enables authentication with the OpenID protocol.

Default templates

There are no default templates provided for the OpenID module.

Default stylesheets

There is one stylesheet dedicated to the OpenID module, located at: `/modules/openid`.

File	Description
`openid.css`	Provides selectors specific to authentication with the OpenID system.
`openid-rtl.css`	A stylesheet that is used when the site employs right-to-left text orientation.

Themable functions

There are no additional themable functions associated with the OpenID module.

Theming the Overlay module

The Overlay module provides the admin system overlay.

Default templates

There are no default templates provided for the Overlay module.

Default stylesheets

There are two stylesheets dedicated to the Overlay module, located at: `/modules/overlay`.

File	Description
`overlay-child.css`	Selectors for the tabs, titles, and controls on the overlay elements.
`overlay-patent.css`	Basic overlay selectors.

Themable functions

There is only one themable function associated with the Overlay module.

Function	Path	Description
`theme_overlay_ disable_message`	`modules/overlay/overlay. module`	Formats the message containing instructions for how to disable the overlay.

Theming the Poll module

Controls the formatting and display of the Poll module, including the voting forms and the results.

Default templates

There are five dedicated templates for the poll functionality, covering block and page output:

- poll-bar--block.tpl.php
- poll-bar.tpl.php
- poll-results--block.tpl.php
- poll-results.tpl.php
- poll-vote.tpl.php

The default templates are located at modules/poll/.

poll-bar--block.tpl.php

Provides a template for formatting the results bar of a single poll answer choice, applicable when poll is in block position. The available variables include:

Variable	Description
$percentage	The percentage of total votes received by this answer choice.
$title	The title of the poll.
$total_votes	The number of votes cast for this answer choice.
$vote	The current user's vote on the poll.
$voted	Returns True if the user had voted on this poll.
$votes	The total number of votes cast in the poll.

poll-bar.tpl.php

Displays the bar for a single choice in the poll. The available variables are the same as those for the template poll-bar-block.tpl.php, above.

poll-results.tpl.php

Provides a template for the display of poll results. The available variables include:

Variable	Description
$cancel_form	The form for a user to cancel their vote.
$links	Links in the poll.
$nid	The NID of the poll.
$raw_links	Raw array of links in the poll.
$results	The results of the poll.
$title	The title of the poll.
$vote	The current user's vote on the poll.
$votes	The total number of votes cast in the poll.

poll-results--block.tpl.php

Provides a template for the display of poll results, applicable in block position. The available variables are the same as those for poll-results.tpl.php.

poll-vote.tpl.php

Provides a template for the voting form for a poll. The available variables include:

Variable	Description
$block	Returns True if this is being displayed in a block.
$choice	The radio buttons for voting on the choices in the poll.
$rest	A catch-all to pick up anything else that may have been added via hooks.
$title	The title of the poll.
$vote	The **vote** button.

Default stylesheets

Two stylesheets are dedicated to the formatting of the Poll module. Both are located at /modules/poll.

File	Description
poll.css	Styling for Polls.
poll-rtl.css	A stylesheet that is used when the site employs right-to-left text orientation.

Themable functions

There are no additional themable functions associated with the Poll module.

Theming the Profile module

The Profile module deals with the user profile pages.

Default templates

Drupal 7 provides three dedicated template files to assist with formatting the profile functionality:

- `profile-block.tpl.php`
- `profile-listing.tpl.php`
- `profile-wrapper.tpl.php`

The default templates are located at `modules/profile/`.

profile-block.tpl.php

Handles the display of a user's profile within a block. The available variables include:

Variable	Description
`$field_title`	The title of the profile field.
`$field_type`	The type of the profile field.
`$field_value`	The value of the profile field.
`$profile`	Array of all profile fields that have data.
`$user_picture`	The image associated with the user.

profile-listing.tpl.php

Provides a template for the user information on the member listing page. The available variables include:

Variable	Description
`$account`	User's account object.
`$field_title`	The title of the profile field.
`$field_type`	The type of the profile field.
`$field_value`	The value of the profile field.
`$name`	The name of the user.

Variable	Description
`$user_picture`	The image associated with the user.
`$profile`	Array of all profile fields that have data.

profile-wrapper.tpl.php

The template that is used for displaying a list of users. The available variables include:

Variable	Description
`$content`	The user account profiles.
`$current_field`	The field being browsed.

Default stylesheets

There is only one stylesheet dedicated to the profile functionality.

File	Description
`profile.css`	There are only three selectors here for the profile fields.

Themable functions

There is only one themable function that relates to the profile functionality.

Function	Path	Description
`theme_profile_admin_overview`	`modules/profile/profile.admin.inc`	Themes the profile field overview.

Theming the Search module

The Search module powers the various search options for Drupal.

Default templates

There are three default templates for theming the search forms:

- `search-block-form.tpl.php`
- `search-result.tpl.php`
- `search-results.tpl.php`

The default templates are located at `modules/search/`.

search-block-form.tpl.php

Provides a template for displaying a search form within a block. The available variables include:

Variable	Description
$search	The complete search form.
$search_form	An array of search form elements.
$search['hidden']	Handles hidden form elements.
$search['search_block_form']	Formats the text input area.
$search['submit']	Handles the form submit button.

search-result.tpl.php

This template renders a single search result. The available variables include:

Variable	Description
$classes-array	Array of HTML class attributes, flattened into a string within the variable $classes.
$content_attributes_array	An array of HTML attributes for the content.
$info	String of all the meta information.
$info_split	Contains the same data as $info, but it is split into an array.
$info_split['comment']	Number of comments.
$info_split['date']	Last update of the node.
$info_split['type']	The node type.
$info_split['upload']	Number of attachments.
$info_split['user']	Author of the node.
$module	The machine-readable name of the module being searched.
$title	The title of the result.
$title_attributes_array	Array of HTML attributes for the title.
$title_prefix	An array of additional output that is displayed in front of the main title tag.
$title_suffix	An array of additional output that is displayed after the main title tag.

Variable	Description
$type	The type of search.
$url	The URL of the result.

search-results.tpl.php

Provides a template for rendering the set of search results. The available variables include:

Variable	Description
$search_results	All results.
$module	The machine-readable name of the module.

Default stylesheets

Two stylesheets are dedicated to the formatting of the search functionality. Both are located at /modules/search.

File	Description
search.css	Styling for the Search module.
search-rtl.css	A stylesheet that is used when the site employs right-to-left text orientation.

Themable functions

There are no additional themable functions associated with the search function.

Theming the Shortcut module

The Shortcut module handles the shortcuts functionality associated with the toolbar area of the admin system.

Default templates

There are no default templates provided for the Shortcut module.

Default stylesheets

File	Description
shortcut.admin.css	Two basic selectors affecting shortcut display.
shortcut.css	The primary stylesheet for formatting the shortcuts.

Themable functions

There is only one themable function associated with the Shortcut module.

Function	Path	Description
theme_shortcut_set_customiza	modules/shortcut/shortcut.admin.inc	Provides the formatting for the shortcut set customization form.

Theming the System module

The System module plays an important role in Drupal. The module provides important functionality for generating pages as well as handling the various configuration controls that help administrators modify the workings of the site.

Default templates

The System module contains some of the most important templates in Drupal. The page and box templates are two key files for theming your site.

- html.tpl.php
- maintenance-page.tpl.php
- page.tpl.php
- region.tpl.php

The default templates are located at: modules/system/.

html.tpl.php

Provides a template for providing essential information included in all themes, for example, the namespace.

Variable	Description
$classes	Classes used to provide contextual CSS styling.
$css	An array of the CSS files for the current page.

Variable	Description
$grddl_profile	A GRDDL profile to be used for extracting RDF data.
$head	The markup for the <head> section.
$head_title	The page title, for use in the TITLE tag.
$head_title_array	Contains the parts used to generate the $head_title variable.
$language	The language the site is displayed in.
$page	The rendered page content.
$page_bottom	Closing markup from any modules that have altered the page.
$page_top	Markup from modules that have altered the page.
$rdf_namespaces	The RDF namespace prefixes.
$scripts	Loads the JavaScript files.
$styles	To import all the CSS files for the page.

maintenance-page.tpl.php

Provides a template for formatting the "site under maintenance" page. The available variables are the same as those applicable to the html.tpl.php and the page.tpl. php files.

page.tpl.php

Provides an important template for controlling the output on a Drupal page. The available variables include:

Variable	Description
$action_links	An array of actions local to the page.
$base_path	The base path of the Drupal installation.
$breadcrumb	The breadcrumb trail for the current page.
$directory	The directory where the theme is located.
$feed_icons	A string of the feed icons relevant to the page.
$front_page	The URL of the front page.
$is_admin	Returns True is user is an administrator.
$is_front	Returns True if current page is the front page.
$logged_in	Returns True if user is logged in and authenticated.
$logo	The path to the logo image.
$main_menu	An array of the main menu links.
$messages	The status and error messages.

Variable	Description
$node	The node object.
$page['content']	A region, in this case, the main content area.
$page['footer']	A region, in this case, the footer region.
$page['header']	A region, in this case, the header region.
$page['help']	A region, in this case, the region that displays the help messages.
$page['highlighted']	A region, in this case, the highlighted content region.
$page['sidebar_first']	A region, in this case, the first sidebar.
$page['sidebar_second']	A region, in this case, the second sidebar.
$secondary_menu	An array containing the secondary menu links.
$site_name	The name of the site, as defined in the admin system.
$site_slogan	The site slogan, as defined in the admin system.
$tabs	The tabs linking to sub-pages (for example, **edit**).
$title	The page title.
$title_prefix	An array of additional output that is displayed in front of the main title tag.
$title_suffix	An array of additional output that is displayed after the main title tag.

region.tpl.php

Provides a template for creating a box around items. The available variables include:

Variable	Description
$classes	Classes used to provide contextual CSS styling.
$classes-array	Array of HTML class attributes, flattened into a string within the variable $classes.
$content	The content for the region (typically blocks).
$is_admin	Returns True when the current user is the admin user.
$is_front	Returns True when the current page is the front page.
$logged_in	Returns True when the current user is logged in and authenticated.
$region	The name of the region variable.

Default stylesheets

There are a large number of stylesheets associated with the System module, however, the primary styling of the key templates discussed above is typically managed from within the `styles.css` file located in the `theme` directory. The following stylesheets are located at: `modules/system`.

File	Description
`system.admin.css`	Contains the styles for the administration pages.
`system.admin-rtl.css`	A stylesheet that is used when the site employs right-to-left text orientation.
`system.base.css`	The Drupal system's theme agnostic styles.
`system.base-rtl.css`	A stylesheet that is used when the site employs right-to-left text orientation.
`system.maintenance.css`	The styles for the maintenance page.
`system-menus.css`	Covers a wide variety of common styles, and also includes menus, tabs, and progress bars.
`system-menus-rtl.css`	A stylesheet that is used when the site employs right-to-left text orientation.
`system.messages.css`	Styling for the system messages.
`system.theme.css`	Basic styling for common markup.
`system.theme-rtl.css`	A stylesheet that is used when the site employs right-to-left text orientation.

Themable functions

There are a number of themable functions that relate to the System module. The functions can be found in two files: `modules/system/system.module` and `modules/system/system.admin.inc`.

Function	Path	Description
`theme_admin_block`	`modules/system/system.admin.inc`	Handles the admin system block display.
`theme_admin_block_content`	`modules/system/system.admin.inc`	Formats the contents of the admin block.
`theme_admin_page`	`modules/system/system.admin.inc`	Formats the administration page.
`theme_confirm_form`	`modules/system/system.module`	Formats the confirmation form.

Function	Path	Description
theme_exposed_filters	modules/system/system.module	HTML for the exposed filters form.
theme_status_report	modules/system/system.admin.inc	Themes the admin system's status report page.
theme_system_admin_index	modules/system/system.admin.inc	Formats the output of the admin dashboard page.
theme_system_compact	modules/system/system.module	Formats the link to show or hide the help descriptions.
theme_system_date_time_settings	modules/system/system.admin.inc	Formats the date setting form.
theme_system_modules_fieldset	modules/system/system.admin.inc	HTML for the modules form.
theme_system_modules_incompatible	modules/system/system.admin.inc	The HTML for the message warning of incompatible modules.
theme_system_modules_uninstall	modules/system/system.admin.inc	Formats the table containing the uninstalled modules.
theme_system_powered_by	modules/system/system.module	Format the **Powered by Drupal** text.
theme_system_settings_form	modules/system/system.module	The HTML for the system settings form.
theme_system_themes_page	modules/system/system.admin.inc	HTML for the Theme Manager page.

Theming the Taxonomy module

The Taxonomy module enables the organization of content into categories, according to a hierarchical vocabulary.

Default Template

The Taxonomy module contains only one dedicated template.

- taxonomy-term.tpl.php

taxonomy-term.tpl.php

Provides a template for creating a box around items. The available variables include:

Variable	Description
$classes	Classes used to provide contextual CSS styling.
$classes-array	Array of HTML class attributes, flattened into a string within the variable $classes.
$content	An array of the content of the term.
$id	Position of a term.
$is_admin	Returns True when the current user is the admin user.
$is_front	Returns True when the current page is the front page.
$logged_in	Returns True when the current user is logged in and authenticated.
$name	The name of the term.
$page	Flag indicating full page state.
$term	The full term object.
$term_url	The URL of the term.
$view_mode	The view mode (teaser, full, and so on).
$zebra	Provides an "odd/even" marker useful for styling.

Default stylesheets

There is one stylesheet dedicated to the Taxonomy module; it is located at:
modules/taxonomy.

Variable	Description
taxonomy.css	Provides four selectors for the taxonomy module.

Themable functions

There are no unique themable functions in the Taxonomy module.

Theming the Toolbar module

The Toolbar module provides the admin system's toolbar functionality.

Default templates

There is no default template provided for the Toolbar module.

Default stylesheets

There is one stylesheet dedicated to the Toolbar module; it is located at: `modules/toolbar`.

File	Description
`toolbar.css`	Provides the selectors for theming the toolbar.

Themable functions

There are no themable functions dedicated to the Toolbar module.

Theming the Tracker module

The Tracker module enables the tracking of recent posts from users.

Default templates

There is no default template provided for the Tracker module.

Default stylesheets

There is one stylesheet dedicated to the Tracker module; it is located at: `modules/tracker`.

File	Description
`tracker.css`	Provides two selectors for theming the tracker table.

Themable functions

There are no themable functions dedicated to the Tracker module.

Theming the Update module

The Update module checks for available updates to the Drupal core and modules and notifies the administrator if any are available.

Default templates

There are no default templates dedicated to the update functionality.

Default stylesheets

Two stylesheets are dedicated to the formatting of the update functionality.
Both are located at `/modules/update`.

File	Description
`update.css`	Numerous selectors for the update module interface in the admin system.
`update-rtl.css`	A stylesheet that is used when the site employs right-to-left text orientation.

Themable functions

There are two themable functions associated with the update functionality.
The functions can be found at: `modules/update/update.report.inc`, `modules/update/update.module`, and at `modules/update/update.manager.inc`.

Function	Path	Description
`theme_update_last_check`	`modules/update/update.module`	The HTML for the last time the system checked for updates.
`theme_update_manager_update_form`	`modules/update/update.manager.inc`	Formats the first page in the update manager wizard (select projects).
`theme_update_report`	`modules/update/update.report.inc`	Formats the project status report.
`theme_status_label`	`modules/update/update.report.inc`	Formats the label to display the update status.
`theme_update_version`	`modules/update/update.report.inc`	Formats the version display.

Theming the User module

Enables the user registration and login system.

Default templates

Theming the user pages is made easier in Drupal 7 through the addition of four dedicated template files:

- `user-picture.tpl.php`
- `user-profile-category.tpl.php`
- `user-profile-item.tpl.php`
- `user-profile.tpl.php`

The default templates are located at: `modules/user/`.

user-picture.tpl.php

Handles the presentation of the image associated with the user's account. The available variables include:

Variable	Description
`$account`	An array of the account information.
`$user_picture`	The image set by the user for the account.

user-profile-category.tpl.php

Provides a template for formatting the presentation of user profiles in category view. The available variables include:

Variable	Description
`$attributes`	The HTML attributes.
`$profile_items`	All the items for the group.
`$title`	The category title for the group.

user-profile-item.tpl.php

Handles the presentation of the user profile data. Loops through to present each item. The available variables include:

Variable	Description
`$attributes`	The HTML attributes.
`$title`	The field title for the profile item.
`$value`	The value for the profile item.

user-profile.tpl.php

Provides a template for presenting all the user data. The available variable:

Variable	Description
$user_profile	All of the user's profile data.

Default stylesheets

Two stylesheets are dedicated to the formatting of the user data. Both are located at `/modules/user`.

File	Description
user.css	Styles for the User module and Profile module, includes styles for user administration.
user-rtl.css	A stylesheet that is used when the site employs right-to-left text orientation.

Themable functions

There are a number of themable functions that relate to the user functionality. The functions can be found in two files: `modules/user/user.module` and `modules/user/user.admin.inc`.

Function	Path	Description
theme_user_admin_permissions	modules/user/user.admin.inc	Themes the permissions manager.
theme_user_admin_roles	modules/user/user.admin.inc	Handles the **new role** form.
theme_user_list	modules/user/user.module	Produces a list of users.
theme_user_permission_description	modules/user/user.admin.inc	Formats individual permission description.
theme_user_signature	modules/user/user.module	Handles the output of the user's signature.

Index

Thank you for buying
Drupal 7 Themes

About Packt Publishing

Packt, pronounced 'packed', published its first book "*Mastering phpMyAdmin for Effective MySQL Management*" in April 2004 and subsequently continued to specialize in publishing highly focused books on specific technologies and solutions.

Our books and publications share the experiences of your fellow IT professionals in adapting and customizing today's systems, applications, and frameworks. Our solution based books give you the knowledge and power to customize the software and technologies you're using to get the job done. Packt books are more specific and less general than the IT books you have seen in the past. Our unique business model allows us to bring you more focused information, giving you more of what you need to know, and less of what you don't.

Packt is a modern, yet unique publishing company, which focuses on producing quality, cutting-edge books for communities of developers, administrators, and newbies alike. For more information, please visit our website: www.packtpub.com.

About Packt Open Source

In 2010, Packt launched two new brands, Packt Open Source and Packt Enterprise, in order to continue its focus on specialization. This book is part of the Packt Open Source brand, home to books published on software built around Open Source licences, and offering information to anybody from advanced developers to budding web designers. The Open Source brand also runs Packt's Open Source Royalty Scheme, by which Packt gives a royalty to each Open Source project about whose software a book is sold.

Writing for Packt

We welcome all inquiries from people who are interested in authoring. Book proposals should be sent to author@packtpub.com. If your book idea is still at an early stage and you would like to discuss it first before writing a formal book proposal, contact us; one of our commissioning editors will get in touch with you.

We're not just looking for published authors; if you have strong technical skills but no writing experience, our experienced editors can help you develop a writing career, or simply get some additional reward for your expertise.

Flash with Drupal

ISBN: 978-1-847197-58-0 Paperback: 380 pages

Build dynamic, content-rich Flash CS3 and CS4 applications for Drupal 6

1. Learn to integrate Flash applications with Drupal CMS

2. Explore a new approach where Flash and HTML components are intermixed to provide a hybrid Flash-Drupal architecture

3. Build a custom audio and video player in Flash and link it to Drupal

Drupal 7 Social Networking: RAW

ISBN: 978-1-849516-00-6 Paperback: 323 pages

Build a social or community website with friends lists, groups, custom user profiles, and much more

1. Step-by-step instructions for putting together a social networking site with Drupal 7

2. Customize your Drupal installation with modules and themes to match the needs of almost any social networking site

3. Allow users to collaborate and interact with each other on your site

Please check **www.PacktPub.com** for information on our titles

CPSIA information can be obtained at www.ICGtesting.com
Printed in the USA
LVOW11s0833110713

342295LV00002B/8/P